ASPECTS OF CALDERDALE

Aspects of Calderdale

DISCOVERING LOCAL HISTORY

Edited by
JOHN BILLINGSLEY

Series Editor
Brian Elliott

Wharncliffe Books

First Published in 2002 by
Wharncliffe Books
an imprint of
Pen and Sword Books Limited,
47 Church Street, Barnsley,
South Yorkshire. S70 2AS

Copyright © Wharncliffe Books 2002

For up-to-date information on other titles produced under the
Wharncliffe imprint, please telephone or write to:

> **Wharncliffe Books**
> **FREEPOST**
> **47 Church Street**
> **Barnsley**
> **South Yorkshire S70 2BR**
> **Telephone (24 hours): 01226 - 734555**

ISBN: 1-903425-20-4

A CIP catalogue record of this book is available from the
British Library

Cover illustration: Nathan Fielding's 'View of Halifax from Haley Hill'

Printed in the United Kingdom by
CPI UK

CONTENTS

INTRODUCTION

by

John Billingsley

WHARNCLIFFE BOOKS *ASPECTS* SERIES of local history publications has already proved popular in a number of towns and districts in northern England, and has now arrived in Calderdale. In this series, we aim to strike a balance of tone, making local history writing both interesting to the established local researcher and also accessible to the growing numbers of people seeking greater knowledge of their place of residence or upbringing. In time, we hope, many of those will come to make their own contributions to the wealth of local history material already available in our borough.

In this volume, I have asked writers to deal with a variety of topics bearing on the character of Calderdale. Michael Haigh sets the scene by recalling our most distant predecessors in the valley, those in prehistory who passed through and then settled within the boundaries of modern Calderdale. They were the first to begin shaping our landscape, a process that has continued with little interruption to the present day.

The most striking changes to the Calder valley, however, occurred much more recently, in the steady march of industry across our green vales and hills. David Nortcliffe describes how quickly and methodically the village of Brighouse expanded to take in its surrounding farmland, in particular on its northern fringes, in its development into the town of today.

Even though one knows full well the pace of urban development in our area, it is always something of a shock to see early maps and pictures revealing green fields where not even a memory remains of such rustic atmosphere. Our cover picture, extracted from Fielding's *View of Halifax from Haley Hill*, is one such shock. Its biggest surprise, however, lies in the matter of its attribution. Is it really as early as has long been supposed? Nigel Herring has put on his detective's hat to find out!

One of the things that upper Calderdale is justly renowned for is its vernacular architecture. In the seventeenth century, many wealthy clothiers rebuilt their houses in stone, preserving for future generations modes of building and patterns of decoration that are almost unique to the area. An especially rich heritage is found in the external decoration of our early stone houses, and David Cant discusses the fascinating variety of designs found in window mouldings of the time.

The dynamic growth of Calderdale's towns obviously necessitated social facilities to answer needs beyond housing and employment. Peter Robinson recognises the appeal of good ale in his description of the vicissitudes of Northowram's James Alderson's involvement in brewing and imbibing in Halifax. The local methods of brewing and abundance of local beers - 'real ale' when there was nothing else - are a far cry from today's national enterprises and their anodyne products.

Some of Alderson and his contemporaries' setbacks were a result of the Victorian reaction to drunkenness, which sparked the Temperance Movement. It was this campaign that led to support among the British people at home for Africans resisting the inroads of unbridled capitalist expansion into their territories. Jill Robinson describes a little-known episode occurring in Halifax in 1895, when three tribal chieftains received a warm welcome in the town.

Temperance and popular resistance came together again in the life of Benjamin Wilson, a Salterhebble man whose early commitment to armed Chartism mellowed over the years. As J A Hargreaves demonstrates, however, his dedication to the cause of the working classes remained constant until the end.

Making waves of a different kind was a remarkable Hebden Bridge woman, Alice Longstaff, who as a teenager opted into the world of photography. Issy Shannon describes her long career as the town photographer, present at important events in personal lives and building a personal collection of local photographs that remains a historical asset to the area.

Communities, whatever their economic standing, are far poorer without folklore and custom. At one time, villages and towns all over Yorkshire and elsewhere had their maypole as a focus for the celebration of the changing seasons, and they were still being erected in the nineteenth century. Warley's new pole was not warmly welcomed by all, however, some people evidently fearing its effect on local sobriety. Garry Stringfellow has investigated for us the rise and fall of Calderdale's best-known maypole.

Public libraries provide the link between the different forms of culture in society, and Derek Bridge here describes their development in our borough from a handful of semi-public institutions to the integrated information service, with outposts in every community, that is aspired to today.

Libraries and literature are of course inseparable, and a number of remarkable literary characters, whose works are still accessible on our library shelves, have lived in our district. Aidan Whelan tells us of the rollercoaster career of one of the nineteenth-century's most popular dialect poets, John Hartley, whose prodigious output included the annual *Clock Almanack* and a number of poetic rebukes to the abuse of power and prestige.

Perhaps Calderdale's most famous literary star, however, is the late Poet Laureate, Ted Hughes. John Billingsley shows how Hughes' poetry reveals a map of his formative years in Mytholmroyd. Reading his work, one realises how much the landscape of the upper Calder valley has affected not only Hughes, but all those within it, acquiring thereby a social meaning of its own.

In Hughes we return to the primal energy of the moors and are left in a world of broken mills and walls predated by the worn-down earthworks of prehistory. We end this collection, therefore, where we began - looking at the hills and valleys of our district and reflecting on how it is our land around us that has shaped so much of our history, which we hope to explore in further volumes of *Aspects of Calderdale*.

If you would be interested in contributing to a further volume of *Aspects of Calderdale*, please contact me at 10 Jubilee Street, Mytholmroyd, Hebden Bridge, West Yorkshire HX7 5NP; or by email at johnbillingsley@jubilee10.freeserve.co.uk.

1. The Early Prehistory of Calderdale

by Michael R Haigh

THE PREHISTORY OF CALDERDALE was determined by its landscape - a raised escarpment of gritstone, cut through by numerous deep valleys. These sheltered valleys, coupled with the relative low heights of the hills in this area, make this an ideal place to cross the Pennines. Major routes have been established since at least the Bronze Age. Much of the land was poor for farming, especially on the western highlands, and the weather made it worse. Where reasonable land does exist, mostly to the east, it has been subject to agricultural improvement to this day.

Palaeolithic Calderdale

Prehistoric cultures are named after the characteristic style of surviving artefacts. The earliest humans used simple but functional tools made of stone. This early time is known as the Paleolithic or Old Stone Age, which ended after the last Ice Age. There appears to be no evidence that humans lived here before the Ice Ages. Although the Upper Calder Valley appears to have been unglaciated, it was close enough to the ice sheets to discourage visitors. Calderdale at this time was a bleak tundra landscape. Although it is possible that Palaeolithic hunters wandered into this district as they followed herds of reindeer, they left nothing to serve as an unambiguous sign of their presence. A few flint blades, which might date from the Upper Palaeolithic, have been found on Midgley Moor, but there is doubt about this.[1] As the ice sheets retreated and the climate improved, the Pennine hills became covered in woodland. Fossilised tree roots, remains of these early forests, can still be seen in parts of the district, notably Cragg Vale.

Mesolithic Calderdale

As the weather improved, bands of hunter-gatherers moved onto the Pennine Hills. They took advantage of various technological improvements to produce a wider range of more sophisticated and versatile tools. These developments allowed early humans to expand into new environments. This era is known as the Mesolithic, or Middle Stone Age, which is sub-divided into an early and a more diverse late phase. Evidence of their presence is scattered over our moors in the form of lost or discarded flint. Most of the flint tools recovered were missile weapons of one sort or another, indicating that game hunting was the main reason for venturing into the district.

A site typical of the early Mesolithic is to be found near the border of Calderdale at Nab Water.[2] This site is located along the crest of a low spur near to the source of the Nab Water stream, about eleven kilometres (seven miles) north-west of Halifax. Here is a place near a dependable source of clean water with good views of the movement of game animals. Sites like this were probably occupied seasonally; people arrived in the summer, following herds of animals such as red deer. During the autumn they returned to their winter sites, which are thought to be on the Coal Measures and Magnesium Limestone terraces which fringe the eastern edge of the Pennines.[3] Most of the evidence found at the site consisted of fragments of discarded flint, indicating a range of activities carried out here, including food preparation, hide processing and the manufacture of wood and bone implements. Few finished tools were found, as these would have been taken by the group when they departed. The flint itself seems to have come from the east coast of Yorkshire. It is not known if there were any structures on the site due to the haphazard excavation techniques of early antiquarians. An excavation at Deepcar in South Yorkshire uncovered a semi-circular structure made of stone. The flints associated with this building were similar to those found at Nab Water, so it is possible that there were some temporary structures here. The finding of burnt flints indicates the presence of hearths.[4]

Mesolithic flints are found scattered all over the hills in Calderdale and the surrounding district. Sometimes these random finds can illuminate a lost moment of Mesolithic life. One such object was the remains of an axe found in 1923, on the bed of Ringstone Edge reservoir, Rishworth. It was constructed from a poor-quality grey flint, with a large hollow inside a cherty area, a flaw not apparent when work started on the tool. When the hollow was exposed, the tool had to be discarded, no doubt accompanied by a choice mesolithic expletive.[5]

The Neolithic.
This was a time of both technological and social change. It was the technological improvements that led to this period becoming known as the Neolithic, or New Stone Age, but this was also the period when farming was introduced and the first large monuments were constructed.

The Wolds of East Yorkshire, an early centre of farming communities, was rich in farmland and exchangeable raw materials, including Whitby jet and flint. From here, it is thought, farming techniques spread across the Vale of York and, eventually, on to the Pennines. Agriculture probably spread into Calderdale from the east, but ploughing and the Industrial Revolution destroyed most of the evidence in the lower valley.

All over the country, the transition to farming took a long time and many people continued to follow hunter/gatherer lifestyles alongside the early tillers and pastoralists. This was especially true in areas like west Calderdale, which had mostly poor soils and climate. Consequently, these hills continued to be used for hunting. These hunters, however, benefited from improvements in stone technology. They used a variety of implements including bows and arrows, tipped with distinctive leaf-shaped arrowheads. Many Neolithic hunter/gatherers used sites first used in the Mesolithic (Figure 1).

There is evidence that that at least one group tried a more permanent form of settlement. Excavation at Holdsworth, near Halifax, uncovered the remains of a rude dwelling.[6] All that remained of the structure were two parallel ditches about 5 metres (16ft 6ins) apart, which held a series of vertical timbers. The gaps between them were presumably filled by either stacks of turf or split timbers. The ditches turned in at the ends, leaving an entrance of about 1.25 m (4 ft) across. The remains of flint working were found around the structure. It is not clear if this was a base for hunting or a genuine

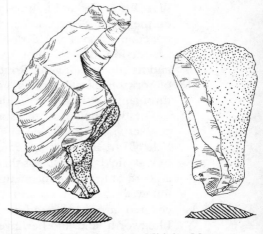

Figure 1. Flints found on Midgley Moor (actual size). *R Law (Roth 1906:290)*

attempt at early farming in the area. However, three Neolithic axeheads have been found in the area, which hint at the fact that land was being cleared for agriculture. Most of these axeheads date from the middle to late part of the Neolithic.

Early Bronze Age.

The Neolithic ended around the time the Beaker culture arrived from continental Europe. With the Beaker culture came new lithic styles, such as 'barbed and tanged' arrowheads, and new materials such as bronze. They also introduced new burial rites, which focused more on the individual. Each person was placed in a separate grave, often accompanied by a decorated ceramic vessel known as a beaker.[7] These beakers developed into a number of different styles, including the collared urn, commonly found in this area. Collared urns were in use from around 2150 to 1600 BCE.[8]

This was a time of climatic improvement that allowed farmers to colonise land further up the Pennine hills. These agriculturists also built small ritual monuments for themselves; some of which have survived. Bronze Age burials in this area generally fall into one of three types: individual burial cairns, earthwork rings and flat cemeteries.

There are moreover indications of long-distance exchange systems. To the east, on the rich farmland of the Yorkshire Wolds, a prosperous society had developed, its wealth based both on natural resources like flint, Whitby Jet and Baltic Amber (which could be found washed up on the North Sea coasts) and agricultural surpluses. To the west lay the copper mines of Alderley Edge in Cheshire and the Great Orme, Llandudno. Beyond these lay the rich megalithic culture of Ireland and its supplies of gold. Routes linking these places crossed the Vale of York on glacial moraines before traversing the Pennines, either through the Aire gap or Calderdale.

The distribution of the surviving ritual sites seems to follow the courses of the proposed trade routes.[9] The suggested way crosses the Vale of York and enters the region from the direction of either Leeds or Wakefield. From Leeds the trail enters Calderdale via Shelf, where a hoard of bronze implements were found in 1856. It then, perhaps, followed the high ground to the north of Halifax. An inverted collared urn was found in a stone cist at Mount Zion chapel, Illingworth, and another inverted urn was discovered at Mixenden church. There may have been a southern route to Halifax following the course of the River Calder from the Wakefield area.

At one time, it was thought that the river and marshland in the valley bottoms would prove impenetrable to early people, but recently a number of serviceable boats dating from the Bronze Age have been found lower down the river around Ferriby, on the Humber estuary. Archaeologists have also uncovered raised wooden walkways crossing marshy ground such as the famous Sweet Track near Glastonbury in Somerset. On an eminence south of the Calder at Rastrick, there was a flat cemetery consisting of about twenty urns, surrounded by the presumed remains of funeral pyres. Further along the valley at Halifax, another flat cemetery consisting of only three inverted urns was discovered at Skircoat.

Beyond Halifax, the trail splits. One branch follows the course of the Ryburn valley, passing the cairn circle on Ringstone Edge on its way to the cluster of sites around Oldham. The other route continues up the Calder Valley, passing through Warley, where a flat cemetery of at least four urns was discovered during the nineteenth century. Beyond Warley lies the cluster of ritual sites around Mytholmroyd. After Mytholmroyd, the route crosses the Hebden and passes Standing Stone Hill outside Heptonstall before there is another split. One trail then heads north through the Widdop gap, passing the small stone circle which surrounded a cremation at Walshaw Dean (Figure 2),[10] before arriving at a large group of sites on Extwistle Moor on the Lancashire side of the Pennines. The other continues to follow the course of the Calder to Todmorden and the important site of the Blackheath Barrow. Beyond that, the route follows the course of the ancient track now called 'The Long Causeway', past the stone circle on Mosley Height and on to another centre of Bronze Age activity around Worsthorne.

It would be wrong to think of these routes as formal tracks traversed by caravans of merchants. They were simple paths linking small farms and communities and may have developed from the old

Figure 2. The restored/reconstructed circle at Walshaw Dean, now embedded in the lining of the reservoir and only occasionally above water. *Michael Haigh*

trails that hunters used to follow game onto the Pennines. A few specialist traders might be active in long-distance commerce, such as the one who hid a collection of tools at Upper Westercroft, Shelf (see below). Most activity, however, was probably the exchange of goods and produce between adjoining localities.

Having discussed the local Bronze Age in general, it is perhaps worth looking at a few of the most interesting sites in more detail. Most surviving remains are of a ritual nature, perhaps because these were built on the edges of communities on land that was always poor for agriculture or building. There are a number of ritual monuments to be found on the moors around Mytholmroyd, possibly forming a ritual landscape. Most of these monuments lie along the southern fringes of Midgley Moor. A number have been destroyed by quarry workings. Those that survive are mostly cairn circles and cairns.

One of the best known is the presumed burial cairn known as 'Miller's Grave' (Figure 3), which consists of a cairn of small rocks heaped over an earthfast boulder. It has been assumed that this pile was erected during the Bronze Age over a noted tribal leader. The mound has been subject to much mutilation over the years.[11] One of the largest monuments is at Cockhill and consists of a large ring of earth and rubble, about 40.3m (132 ft) across. There are traces of an

Figure 3. The mutilated remains of Miller's Grave, Midgley Moor. *Michael Haigh*

internal ditch at the north-west and a central mound, excavated during the 1950s. No indications that it was a burial mound were found, although half a quern was uncovered.[12] At one time at least two other rings could be found nearby, but quarrying destroyed them all.

Although delving has destroyed many sites, new ones are still being discovered here. Within recent years, local antiquarian John Billingsley discovered a new burial mound, ring cairn and several other ancient remains on Midgley Moor (Figure 4).[13] The ring cairn is especially interesting. It consists of a penannual rubble bank, with an orthostatic inner wall. In the south-west quadrant of the circle is what appears to be the remains of a small internal cairn. In many ways it resembles a smaller version of Barbrook II in the Peak District.[14]

Other sites are alleged to have existed at Castle Carr. A lithograph dating from 1842

Figure 4. Hengeiform earth circle on Midgley Moor near Han Royd. *John Billingsley*

purports to show a number of burial mounds scattered around the valley floor (Figure 5).[15] Almost all the features were destroyed when the reservoirs were constructed. though one cairn circle seems to have survived on the southern flank of the second reservoir.[16] The

Figure 5. Barrows at Castle Carr, 1842. *Mr Carter (Roth 1906:306)*

fact that such sites were located on a valley floor shows that Bronze Age people did not necessarily keep to the hills. However, sites built on the popular lowlands are naturally vulnerable to obliteration by later activity.

Another surviving site is the circle on Ringstone Edge near Rishworth. There is little to see nowadays save a patch of darker vegetation, but in former times the rubble bank and standing stones attracted the attention of a number of local antiquarians. Unfortunately, this unskilled delving destroyed much information. It would appear that Ringstone Edge, like the Midgley Moor examples, was originally a circle of cairn material held in place by a ring of standing stones. There are a number of monuments of this type to the south in the Derbyshire Peak District. The site possibly functioned as an arena for rituals. There is evidence, in the form of buried cremations, that it was certainly used as an area for the disposal of dead individuals. At least one urn is known to have been removed before a more systematic investigation was conducted in 1905. This excavation found a cluster of five separate patches of charred wood, interpreted as the remains of funeral pyres. An urn was found, in the remains of a cist, south-west of the circle's centre.[17]

This monument may also have been linked with a collection of seven possible grave mounds noted nearby. It is however possible that these were only agricultural clearance cairns. Also in the vicinity is evidence for Bronze Age settlement. A local antiquarian noted a number of circular settings of stone on the bottom of Ringstone Edge reservoir when the water level was low. Although these could date to any period, a large number of Bronze Age flints have been found in the immediate area.[18]

Apart from these ambiguous observations, little remains to show where Bronze Age people actually lived. The criteria for locating a farm remain the same throughout human history, and so later farms were built on top of Bronze Age settlements. This can be illustrated by the discovery of a stone axe found at Hollins in Warley. It was found about 1.2 m (4 ft) down while the foundations of a barn were being dug.[19] Another theory about where our ancestors actually lived concerns the early history of local religious sites.

One of the most interesting sites in Calderdale is the embanked circle found at Blackheath, near Todmorden (Figure 6). This site was subject to excavation in the final years of the nineteenth century and now forms an unusual hazard on a golf course. Although nothing spectacular was found, there are a number of atypical features about several of the artefacts found here. A metre-wide rubble bank, into

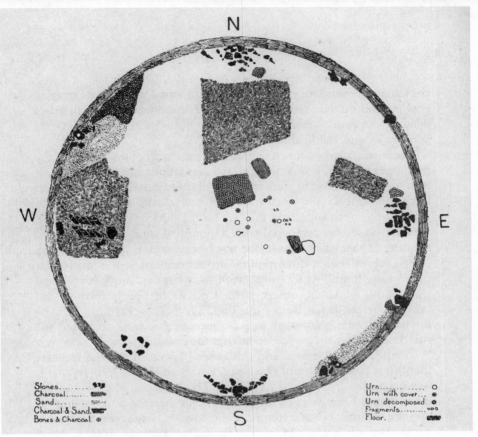

Figure 6. Plan of Blackheath Barrow. *J L Russell? (Roth 1906:308)*

which a number of large stones were set at regular intervals, encircled the site. Curiously, an area of charcoal was found near each of these small monoliths and one even seems to have been blackened by fire. At the centre of the monument was found a buried urn containing the remains of a cremation. This vessel was described as being 'a very fine urn, of elegant form, beautifully proportioned and ornamented with extreme care'.[20] Inside was a small accessory cup containing a bronze knife, bronze pin and bone pin. A ring of deposits surrounded this. Complete urns were found in two of these while the others contained only fragments of urns or were without pottery.

Among this ring of deposits was the enigmatic urn 'No 6' (Figure 7). The first unusual aspect of this pot was that a second smaller vessel had been inverted and placed inside the larger urn, apparently to protect its contents. Inside were the cremated remains of a small woman, around 1.2 m (4 ft) in height. It also

Figure 7. Urns and cup No. 6, Blackheath Barrow. *J L Russell? (Roth 1906:313)*

contained an accessory cup containing a small quantity of greyish powder and the remains of a necklace. This adornment consisted of beads of jet and amber, which have recently been shown to be of Whitby Jet and Baltic amber.[21]

There was a large area of charcoal to the north of the centre of the monument where, it was thought, the cremations had taken place. It is thought that the urns were made on-site. Inside the circle were two large pits, one in the north-east and one to the south-east, from which it has been suggested the clay for the pots was extracted. Each ceramic vessel was tempered with a 'pounded sandstone grit' and a quantity of this was found in the north-west sector.

At each of the cardinal points, the remains of four semicircular cairns were found. At the southernmost, a large quantity of charcoal was found, while the others yielded pieces of poorly formed and broken pottery. It has been suggested that these were kilns for firing the funeral ware,[22] although at least one of those who excavated the site thought that they were 'rude kists for enclosing urns'.[23]

The presence of graves and the general layout of the site indicate that this was an important ritual site, but there are suggestions that it was originally domestic in function.[24] The presence of charcoal and burnt ground are as indicative of domestic hearths and cooking as they are of ritual. When a stone circle at Mosley Height was excavated, a number of household items, including rubbing stones, hand hammers, pot boilers and part of a quern were found under a paved floor. This was interpreted as indicating that the site was a normal home before being converted for religious purposes.[25] It has been

Figure 8. The Bronze Age toolkit from Mixenden. *T D Whittaker (Calderdale Libraries)*

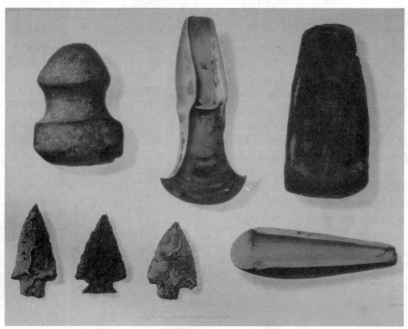

suggested that the site may have been the home of some notable local figure, before being converted into a religious monument.

Although most finds of this period are of a ritual nature, there are discoveries which cast some light on the everyday life of Bronze Age farming folk. One such was unearthed in 1776 by a labourer digging peat on Mixenden Moor. He unearthed a small hoard of ancient tools, consisting of a grooved hammer stone, a bronze palstave axe, a polished stone axe, a stone gouge and arrowheads (Figure 8). This assemblage has been interpreted as the tool kit of a local homesteader.[26] It is possible that the tools were fastened to wooden handles and shafts when they were originally deposited, but these have rotted away. The presence of arrowheads indicates that hunting may well have still provided an important source of protein. The stone axe was probably used for everyday woodcutting jobs like felling trees. Although bronze smelting and casting had been discovered, the metal was an expensive commodity. The bronze palstave found in the hoard was hardly used and may well have been a prestige item, only for show. The hammerstone would have been fastened to a handle and used as any modern hammer, except that there were unlikely to be any metal nails. It may well have been used to hammer wooden stakes into the ground for constructing huts and stock enclosures. The stone gouge is a rare and unusual tool. It may have been used in a variety of specialised wood-carving roles. The tools themselves are, perhaps, most consistent with use by pastoral farmers. There is little evidence for agriculture at this time except perhaps for a stone axe-hammer found at Wainstalls in 1872. Implements of this type are thought to date from around 1650-1250 BCE and could be used as a hoe or as an ard for arable farming.[27]

We can only speculate as to why these tools were deposited here. They may have been hidden during times of trouble to prevent theft, or maybe left here for safekeeping while the owners left the district and did not return. They could also have been buried as a ritual 'sacrifice'.

Another hoard, found in 1856 at Upper Westercroft in Shelf, tells a different story. This deposit was uncovered during quarry-working and consisted of two spearheads and eight axes, all of bronze.[28] The fact that one of the axes was unfinished leads to the conclusion that they were probably the stock-in-trade of an itinerant metalworker.[29]

All the evidence indicates that life in Bronze Age Calderdale was hard. It seems that the improving climate led to people taking advantage of marginal land and gradually spreading up the valley sides, but there is little evidence of any substantial wealth in the area - just small family groups struggling to make a living. The hoards suggest life may have been quite precarious on occasion. As time passed, however, changes came which made this hard life unbearable.

Late Bronze Age.

Towards the end of the Bronze Age the climate went into decline. This led to marginal land, like that in the west of Calderdale, becoming uninhabitable. People were forced to abandon the hills and drift towards the lowlands. By the end of the Late Bronze Age, it is thought, defensive sites were built at Almondbury, near Huddersfield,[30] and at Castercliffe, near Colne. Perhaps these were constructed to control the flow of desperate people trickling down off the Pennines, though we cannot be certain. A few farmers may have managed to hang on, especially in the lower eastern parts. Most, especially those from the hills, appear to have left.

Thus, this survey of the prehistory of Calderdale ends much as it began, with our district largely empty, except perhaps for opportunist hunters and travellers.

Notes and References

1. Faull, M, & Moorhouse, S A (eds). *West Yorkshire: an Archaeological Survey to AD 1500*. West Yorkshire Metropolitan County Council. 1981 (4 Vols), p 75.
2. Gilks, J A. 'Earlier Mesolithic sites at Nab Water, Oxenhope Moor, West Yorkshire'. *Yorkshire Archaeological Journal* (YAJ) Vol 66, 1994, p 1-19.
3. Gilks, 1994. p 17.
4. Gilks, 1994. p 16.
5. Davies, J, & Rankine, W F. 'Mesolithic flint axes from the West Riding of Yorkshire'. *YAJ* Vol 40, 1960.
6. Barnes, Bernard. *Man and the Changing Landscape*. Merseyside County Council/Merseyside County Museums/University of Liverpool Department of Prehistoric Archaeology, 1982. p 115.
7. Mike Parker Pearson in Hunter, J & Ralston, I. *The Archaeology of Britain*. Routledge, 1999, p 77-94.
8. Hunter & Ralston, 1999, p 81.
9. Watson. Geoffrey G. *Early Man in the Halifax District*. Halifax Scientific Society. 1952, p 47-62.
10. Faull and Moorhouse, Vol 1, 1981, p 98
11. Barnes, 1982, p 116.
12. Barnes, 1982, p 118.
13. Billingsley, John & Bennett, Paul. *Northern Earth* 65, Spring 1996.
14. Barnatt, John. The Henges, *Stone Circles and Ringcairns of the Peak District*. Sheffield Archaeological Monographs No 1. Dept of Archaeology and Prehistory, University of Sheffield, 1990, p 55-57.
15. Roth, H Ling. *The Yorkshire Coiners 1767-1783 & notes on old and prehistoric Halifax* (1906) Repub. SR Publishers, 1971, p 306.
16. These remains were pointed out to me by Harry Armitage during a local history walk c.1981.
17. Barnes, 1982, p 114.
18. Watson, 1952, p 61.
19. Roth, 1971, p 298.
20. Russell, in Roth, 1971, p 319.
21. Duncan Thomas, the man who did this analysis, communicated the results during an archaeological lecture, Mar/April 2000.
22. Barnes, 1982, p 117.
23. Roth, 1971, p 310.
24. Watson, 1952, p 61.
25. Watson, 1952, p 61-62.
26. Varley, Raymond A. 'Lost Neolithic and Bronze Age Finds from Mixenden, near Halifax, West Yorkshire'. *YAJ*, Vol 70, 1998, p 25-33, p 29.
27. Varley, Raymond A. 'A Stone Axe-hammer, Robin Hood's Penny Stone and Stone Circle at Wainstalls, Warley Near Halifax, West Yorkshire'. *YAJ*, Vol 69, 1997, p 9-21.
28. Watson, 1952, p 100.
29. Barnes, 1982, p 117.
30. Faull & Moorhouse, Vol 1, 1981, p 116.

2. THE DEVELOPMENT OF NORTH BRIGHOUSE 1790-1910

by David Nortcliffe

Setting the Scene

UNTIL ABOUT 1790, Brighouse was a river crossing and just a few houses. A 1799 map of the central area shows only sixty houses and a corn mill.[1] Administratively it was a 'quarter' of the much larger township of Hipperholme, though in 1846, the '...hamlet of Brighouse' was split off from the rest of the township. That was run by Improvement Commissioners until 1865, and then by a Local Board until 1893, when it became a Borough.[2]

Around 1800 the population of the whole township of Hipperholme, plus the adjoining township of Rastrick, was only 5,000-5,500. By 1900 the comparable figure was around 25,200, i.e. about a five-fold increase overall.[3] However, even a superficial check on maps of the period shows that growth was far from evenly spread across the area. The major expansion was in a linear band through Rastrick, in the central part of Brighouse, and across the area immediately to the north of Brighouse.

Even in 1790, Brighouse and Rastrick had better communications than most adjoining areas - the Calder & Hebble Canal had arrived in 1764 and the Leeds - Elland Turnpike had been built in 1740/1. The railway would arrive in 1840. The area had coal, water (for both waterpower and processing) and building materials. Additionally, some of the population had experience in textile manufacturing. There was also rather more level building land than was the case further west (Figure 1).[4]

Whilst the Brighouse area, like most of the old Parish of Halifax, had had a domestic wool textile industry which was developing into a water-powered industry by 1790, this area would not restrict itself to wool in the nineteenth century. Cotton was introduced in 1792, worsted manufacturing about 1800, and silk in 1843. By 1870 there were sixteen companies in cotton, and seven silk businesses in the town. Equally important was the development and expansion of other industries serving, or allied to, the textile mills. These included carpet manufacture, dyeing, chemical manufacture, boilermakers, the wire industry, tanners, iron-founders, general engineers and

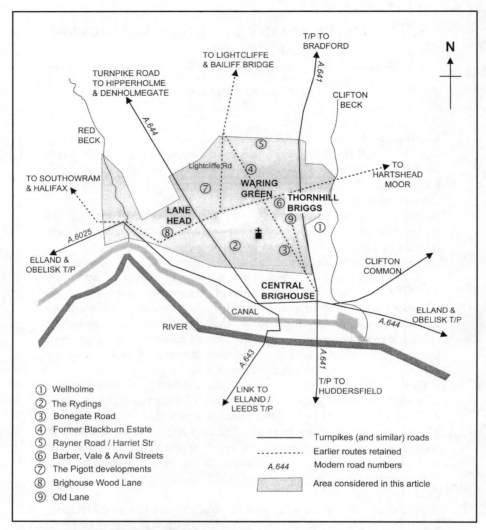

Figure 1. Map of the area covered by this article. *David Nortcliffe.*

valve manufacturers. There were also several quarrying concerns, particularly in Southowram and Hipperholme, able to provide stone for the building boom to come.[5]

These businesses needed space for their mills and they grabbed all available sites on streams, on good building land, near the centre, near existing roads and the canal. The Kirklees Estate sold off approximately 100 acres in the town centre in 1816 and that provided a little more space for new development.[6] However, land at the centre was soon exhausted and developers had to look for other sites in which to expand.

Up to the Mid-1830s

North of Brighouse centre was an area from Brookfoot on the Red Beck, in the west, through Lane Head and Waring Green to Thornhill Briggs, on the Clifton Beck, in the east. These locations were linked by an old route from Halifax and Southowram heading for Hartshead Moor, where it joined another road bound for Wakefield. Where it passed through our study area, it is marked today by Brighouse Wood Lane, Waterloo Road and Thornhill Bridge Lane.

This area was also on an existing cart-road from Brighouse bridge to Bradford via Briggate, Lane Head, Lightcliffe Road, Smith House, Bailiff Bridge and Lower Wyke.[7] Whilst the area included some sloping ground, it was quite suitable for workers' houses. It was also within easy walking distance for the centre of Brighouse, for the cluster of mills developing at Thornhill Briggs, and for those in the lower Red Beck valley at Slead Syke and Brookfoot. Only the seventeenth-century Bonegate Hall and a few scattered farms existed prior to 1790, though the two 'out of town' industrial areas just mentioned were coming into being at that date. Slead Syke Mill (wool textiles) was built around 1790 (Figure 2), the much older corn mill at Brookfoot was rebuilt in 1805 to produce wool cloth,

Figure 2. Slead Syke Mill around the third quarter of the nineteenth century.

and Brookfoot Dye Works came into being in 1807. At Thornhill Briggs there were two cotton mills by the early years of the new century.[8]

In the early 1820s, new turnpike roads helped to open up north Brighouse. The Huddersfield to Low Moor road (now the A641 Bradford Road) was built in 1823, and the Brighouse & Denholmegate Turnpike (now the A644 Halifax Road) opened three years later, linking at Hipperholme to a good road into Halifax. North Brighouse also benefited from the new Elland & Obelisk Turnpike of 1815, passing through Brookfoot, as that provided another link to Halifax and beyond into Lancashire.[9] In conjunction with the pre-existing old roads, by 1830 there was a reasonable road network within north Brighouse and connections to several other areas.

The area gained a certain standing when a new Parish Church was built north of the centre of Brighouse in 1831, funded by the 'Million Pound Act' which created churches in newly expanding industrial areas (Figure 3). In 1835 a National School was built nearby, which still functions as the Adult Education Centre for the town.[10] By this period the central area of the town was becoming full and outward expansion would have to start quite soon.

Figure 3. Brighouse Parish Church and surrounding buildings in the 1840s.

The Early Victorian Years

On the eastern side of our area, Mr Camm, who owned a cotton mill at Thornhill Briggs, had a fine house built nearby at some date just prior to 1836, with an area of parkland in front of it. The Camm house later became three houses, constituting the lower part of the Wellholme cul-de-sac, and Mr Camm's private park was acquired by the town of Brighouse in 1935 as its main park. Despite that expense, Camm could still re-build his cotton mill at Thornhill Briggs in 1859 and was expanding.[11] A map of 1836 shows the existence of the first courts off lower Bonegate Road, though the major developments there would not start for another 30 years.[12]

On the western side, John Brooke, a well-to-do corn miller, built himself a handsome house called The Rydings about 1841 (now the Library) with grounds adjoining the new vicarage which had been built near the Parish Church in 1840.[13] Across the Denholmegate Turnpike from The Rydings, Mr Bottomley built Stoneleigh in 1856, just five years after he had started a dyestuffs and chemical company at Brookfoot.[14] Above those houses, the *Albion Inn* was built in 1853 and the present Post Office in 1854.[15] The Leppington family owned a textile mill at Brookfoot and their new home (now a hotel) was across the corner from the Post Office.[16] On the top side of the Waterloo Road junction was the Toll House for the Turnpike.[17] By 1856, Lane Head was no longer just the head of the old Wood Lane from Brookfoot - it was the focus of an area which would soon be an intensive housing development.

1860 to 1895

This is the thirty-five-year period when the area from the Bradford turnpike road in the east to the Denholmegate turnpike in the west was infilled, mainly with houses for 'the working classes'. However, unless one was wealthy enough to own a riding horse and/or carriage, the only means of travelling to work was on foot, so the middle class also needed to be within walking distance of work and some houses for them are found in this area also. Development started on three fronts - up the Bonegate hillside, along Bradford Road, and beyond Lane Head.

Starting in the central part, Bonegate Road was paved in 1862, permitting better access in preparation for development.[18] The first courts on the east side had been built already, but builders moved in higher up the improved road on land owned by Martin Manley, whose name is perpetuated in Manley Street. That street bears the date 1878 part way along, though it can be shown from map evidence that some was built up before 1875. Manley's estate was sold in 1875 and this released more land for building, with houses springing up on both sides of Bonegate Road.[19] Developers included the local Co-op, which in 1880 built houses forming The Crescent, which were then sold to their members.[20]

Typically, building work started on sites closest to town and worked outwards. But that was not always the case, as some landowners were more ready to sell, or develop land themselves, whilst others held back. Consequently, Kimberley Street (with a datestone 1899 under its former name of Bonegate Place) is over twenty years later than Manley Street, but downhill of it and closer to town. Just above Manley Street, development stopped for a while in the last fifteen years of the century, leaving an open space between there and Waring Green.

Waring Green itself stood at the junction of the improved Bonegate Road with the old Brookfoot/Lane Head/Thornhill Briggs track mentioned earlier. Right on that junction one can still see a datestone 1864 on the corner shop and that seems to have been about the start of building around that crossroads. Just above there, a large area of land, formerly part of the Granny Hall estate owned by Mr Mark Blackburn, was put up for sale in 1870.[21] Soon after, several streets were built on both sides of Bonegate Road. These linked up to the pre-existing farm at Spring Gardens best known as the birthplace of the notable local singer Mrs Sunderland, who is still commemorated in the annual singing competition.[22] Above Waring Green, the first street east of Bonegate Road, and parallel to it, is Marion Street, dated at fairly regular intervals along its length, showing that building work there spanned the years 1881-87.

As it had done over a decade earlier, the Co-op bought some land

Figure 4. Rayner Road, a Co-op development. *David Nortcliffe*

between Bonegate Road and Bradford Road to build long sloping terraces at Rayner Road (Figure 4) and Harriet Street in the early 1890s. Again, these were for sale to their members. Waring Green continued to grow as a separate community with a Co-op store built at the road junction in 1875 (demolished a century later),[23] and a Congregational Chapel near that same junction in 1878. The latter became the Sunday School when a new Chapel was built in 1902 and is now part of the Community Centre.[24]

By 1865 there were already a few houses along the side of the turnpike near the bottom of Bonegate Road. St James' Church was built for the new community, virtually opposite the bottom of Bonegate Road, in 1870.[25] As outward development gained pace, the present pattern of terraces at right-angles to Bradford Road was created between 1875-88. Their names tell us quite a lot about the developers. For example, Hardy and Gathorne Streets perpetuate the names of a leading director of the Low Moor Iron Company. Industrial Street was built by the Co-op (more properly the Brighouse & District Industrial Co-operative Society). The former Co-op store nearby is dated 1888 with a fine carved beehive and globe still in place over the shopfront. Oddfellows Street was financed by the Friendly Society of that name in 1888.[26]

At Thornhills Briggs, house-builders were no doubt encouraged by the erection of the new Woodvale Mills in 1880 by Richard Kershaw (Figure 5). These covered five acres, with 40,000 silk spinning spindles, and employed 600-700 operatives. The main 'A' mill (behind the present Police Station and burnt down in 1985) was just over 100 yards long and four storeys high.[27]

Larger named houses were built at the bottom of each street facing

Figure 5. Woodvale Silk Mills as it was from its construction until its loss by fire.

onto the main road. They are all slightly different, but obviously built for a rather wealthier clientele. So, by 1890, there was continuous housing right along Bradford Road from the bottom of Bonegate Road to Thornhill Briggs. In fact development had actually passed there, as the next street north, Hey Street, is dated 1890.

In the 1880s, development on that eastern side was also creeping up the slope towards Waring Green with the building of Barber Street, Vale Street and Anvil Street. The latter bears two datestones, 1883 and 1888, at different points in the street. Again there are some larger type, double-fronted houses, notably in Vale Street. The area was recognised as having a significant population when, in 1884, St Andrew's School was built in Thornhill Bridge Lane (demolished 1972 and now the site of houses).[28]

A track known as Old Lane ran from the lower part of Bonegate Road to Thornhill Bridge Lane (and still does). Development spread along this axis too: for example, Camm Street there - developed by the family from Wellholme - includes one house dated 1885 showing it to be contemporary with both the Bonegate Road and Bradford Road building works.

Turning to the western side of our area, we have seen how Lane Head existed as a small group of buildings by the early 1860s. A chapel was added in 1864[29] and soon after, housing development started in a big way. Sir Gillery Pigott was a Baron of the Court of Exchequer and owner of the Ashday Hall estate at Southowram. He started developing his land at Lane Head in 1864-65, building hundreds of houses (and shops) in row after row of streets. One street was named after the family, one after his wife Frances and another after his daughter Catherine. Unfortunately, he died in 1875 and his widow, two sons and six daughters mortgaged the estate heavily. Nonetheless, it still continued to be developed right through to the early 1890s - as can be seen from datestones on several rows. Later, when the mortgagee was unable to get money due from the family, he foreclosed and Ashday Hall plus its estate was eventually sold in 1898.[30]

The *Crown Hotel* is contemporary with these houses having been built in 1878.[31] Crown Street is interesting, as the houses are built in blocks with notably different detailing on each block. This whole development, stretching from the present Waterloo Road to Garden Road, appears to have been built in a rolling programme over about thirty years. One of the latest is East View House, dated 1893, now a shop, facing Soothill's Chip Shop in Lightcliffe Road. Pigott's plan involved all streets crossing at right-angles except for Lightcliffe Road, part of the old route to Bradford mentioned earlier. This kept to its original line, winding slightly through the new pattern of streets. On the opposite side of Lightcliffe Road are houses of similar period built on land released by the Blackburn sale of 1870/1 (already mentioned in connection with Bonegate Road developments).

Elsewhere in this western part are a couple of much larger mid-to-late Victorian gentlemen's residences in Brighouse Wood Lane, emphasising the point made earlier that everyone needed to live within walking distance of their work. 'Woodbank' is hidden from view at the end of a long drive and for virtually all of the first half of the twentieth century was the home of G F Sugden of the local flour-milling family.[32] The other house is 'Elmroyd', the onetime home of Theodore Ormerod of H & T T Ormerod, wine & spirit merchants in Briggate (where Tesco is now). He was the third generation to run that business, which had been established in 1760. Much later, in 1921, the Dyers Club bought the house[33] and remained there until the 1980s, when the number of actual dyers got so low that the club was no longer viable. It was then sold off and the land around it became a housing complex.

1895 to 1910
By 1895 the area across the north side of central Brighouse was almost solid housing, most of it having been built in the previous 30 years. Almost the only exception was the south side of Waterloo Road, which was allotments and a football field. By 1913 even the latter was owned by Brookes Ltd of Lightcliffe, who had plans to build a 'Garden City' there, but the advent of World War One caused those plans to be dropped.[34] A little further north, on the extreme edge of this study area, the Garden Road Recreation Ground (originally old delves), consisting of 6.2 acres, was bought by the town in 1895 for £2,800 when the Pigott estate started to be sold off.[35]

Small pockets of housing land remained and these were infilled between 1895-1910. Churchfields Lane, between the former Manley estate of the 1870s and Waring Green, was just a path until it was made up in 1896. Houses were then built along it and the short streets created off it (including on the site of the present car-park near the Parish Church).[36] Kersley Cottages, just below the end of Churchfields Lane, are dated 1902 and they virtually completed the development of Bonegate Road. Below the Parish Church and the 1835 school, a new Girls' Grammar school was built close to the town centre in 1909.[37]

On the eastern side, communications improved in 1903 when

Halifax Corporation built a tram route into Brighouse via Bonegate Road, continuing along Bradford Road to Bailiff Bridge.[38] St Peg Mill was built at Thornhill Briggs in 1909, adding to job opportunities in that sector, and Thornhill Briggs Club was built in 1906 to meet the men's social needs there.[39]

In the Lane Head area, The Rydings and its grounds were bought for the town by public subscription in 1897 to celebrate Queen Victoria's Diamond Jubilee and it opened as a free library in 1898 with some of the old stables used to house the horse-drawn fire engine. The first Mayor of Brighouse, Alderman William Smith, had an Art Gallery extension built onto the library at his own expense and that opened in 1907. He also supplied the first batch of pictures.[40] Across Halifax Road from the bottom of the The Rydings' grounds, an empty plot was filled with a terrace of good quality houses built up flights of steps in 1895. These were designed by Miles Sharp, a local architect and artist who himself moved into No 27.[41] The Lightcliffe Road developments ended at Garden House, near the Bonegate Road / Garden Road junction, which bears a 1901 datestone.

Conclusion

This compact area, roughly half a mile east-west, and rather less than that north-south, was systematically developed for housing, with much of that taking place in the 30 years between 1865-1895. Though the emphasis was on house-building, shops, chapels, pubs, clubs, the library and schools were provided within the new communities.

Many entrepreneurs were involved and many types of house were built. They ranged from back-to-back terraces, through-terraces, and semis to detached houses, which all varied in size as well as type. Few had gardens and sanitary provisions were initially somewhat rudimentary (shared in some cases). All seem to have been provided with running cold water and most had town gas supplies.

Today, their original specification would be seen as sub-standard, yet by the standards of those times they were houses of very reasonable quality. There is good detailing on window and door headers on many houses, good local stone was used and there are some notable architectural features such as the rounded corner houses at the bottom of Lightcliffe Road and an early use of patent glazing at Waring Green Chapel.[42] A century and a quarter later the houses have been modified and improved, converting them into very acceptable homes for the early twenty-first century.

One of the great things about the area is that you can still wander through it today, see how the area grew, why it happened there, and how the area has adapted to changing circumstances in the intervening years.

Bibliography and Notes

1. *History of Brighouse, Rastrick & Hipperholme,* J Horsfall Turner. Idle, 1893.
2. *Brighouse, Portrait of a Town,* R Mitchell. Brighouse, 1953.
3. 'Population of Brighouse, West Yorkshire 1851', M Barke. Yorks. *Archaeological Journal 1976; Brighouse - Birth & Death of a Borough,* R Mitchell. Driffield, 1976.
4. *West Yorkshire: 'A Noble Scene of Industry',* R C N Thornes. Wakefield, 1981.
5. *History of Brighouse and its Co-operative Society,* J Caldwell. Brighouse, 1899; Yorkshire Cotton, G Ingle. Preston, 1997.
6. Mitchell 1953.
7. 'Ancient Highways of the Parish of Halifax IV', W B Crump, *Transactions of the Halifax Antiquarian Society (THAS),* 1925; *Illustrated Rambles from Hipperholme to Tong,* Jas. Parker. Bradford, 1904; *Old Brighouse,* D Rastrick (compiler). Guiseley, 1986.
8. Caldwell 1899; Mitchell 1953.
9. Thornes 1981.
10. *Brighouse Parish Church History,* E I Mack. Brighouse, 1910.
11. Caldwell 1899; 1836 Township map of Hipperholme-cum-Brighouse.
12. Township map, 1836.
13. Mack 1910; *Buildings of Brighouse,* D Nortcliffe. Brighouse, 1978.
14. Letter from QRH Computer Group (then occupying Stoneleigh) to the author, April 1983; *Brighouse Echo* Centenary publication, 26 June 1987.
15. The Post Office has its date inscribed on it; 'Brighouse in the 18th & 19th Centuries', C Jessop. *Brighouse Echo,* Jan 1892.
16. Letter from Ralph Wade to the author, Nov. 2000; Horsfall Turner 1893.
17. Mitchell 1953.
18. Mitchell 1953.
19. D Rastrick (compiler),1986.
20. Caldwell 1899.
21. Letter to *Brighouse Echo,* 16 June 2000, from Mr D Rawlinson, quoting a copy of sale particulars and map in his possession.
22. Horsfall Turner 1893.
23. Caldwell 1899.
24. Mitchell 1953 & 1976.
25. Mack 1910.
26. Caldwell 1899. Also inscribed datestones on buildings there.
27. *Brighouse in old picture postcards,* P Tiler (compiler), Zaltbommel (Netherlands), 1987.
28. *Brighouse Parish Church History 1831-1981,* S Firth. Brighouse, 1981.
29. *History of the Church from 1791,* Geo. Howe. Brighouse, 1978.
30. 'Ashday in Southowram', T Bretton. THAS 1942.
31. Article by C Helme, *Brighouse Echo* 2 June 2000.
32. *The Sugden Story - 150 years of Progress,* R Wade, Brighouse, n.d. (early 1980s).
33. *White's Halifax & Neighbourhood Directory,* Sheffield, 1894; Mitchell 1976.
34. Mitchell, 1953 & 1976.
35. Mitchell, 1976.
36. Mitchell, 1976.
37. Mitchell, 1976.
38. *Halifax in the Tramway Era,* H B Priestley, Sheffield, 1977.
39. Mitchell, 1976.
40. Mitchell, 1976.
41. Information from Stanley Firth, a resident in this row.

3. A QUESTION OF ATTRIBUTION: NATHAN FIELDING AND HIS VIEWS OF HALIFAX FROM HALEY HILL

by Nigel Herring

HISTORIC CERTAINTY must always be a moot point. It is, of course, comforting to think we know the facts, the truth, the answers. However, our assumptions about the past - its events, its characters and even its artifacts - are constantly being challenged. This short paper focuses on one artifact - a late eighteenth century view of Halifax - which twenty years ago appeared to have a well-established pedigree, and solid origins. Today, in the light of fresh evidence, this has to be reconsidered, and the painting's attribution questioned.

Considered both artistically and historically, 'View of Halifax from Haley Hill' (Figure 1) has to be counted as one of the gems of the Calderdale Museums collections. This sizeable oil painting is (or so we thought) the first substantial depiction of Halifax, and with its

Figure 1. 'View of Halifax from Haley Hill. *Calderdale Museums*

bluish suffused atmosphere redolent of the late eighteenth century.

Back in 1974, all this was not immediately apparent. The painting was hanging above the white marble fireplace in the morning room at Bankfield Museum. Sadly, it was in a ruinous condition, with substantial areas of the sky flaking away, and the whole painting suffused in a brownish hue, lending it an old-master appearance. It was nonetheless possible to interpret the main features of the view. The vantage point adopted by the artist was clearly chosen to focus attention on the newly-built North Bridge. In the foreground, one could make out a couple and a child perambulating in a garden with views over the bridge to the town beyond with its huddle of buildings the length of Woolshops and a sprinkling of houses, warehouses and workshops in amongst a semi-rural setting of fields, trees and the enclosing hills.

Bankfield's accession registers recorded the painting as having been donated in 1934 by the daughter of Alderman Whiteley Ward, and stated straightforwardly that it was the work of Nathan Fielding. This appeared to be confirmed by a short piece written by the first curator of Bankfield and published in the *Halifax Naturalist* of 1901.[1] Henry Ling Roth, after listing the principal features of the view, pointed to the fact that the painting had been used as the source for the engraved frontispiece in Jacob's *History of Halifax*, published in 1789 (Figure 2). The engraved version bears the title 'A North-West View of Halifax in Yorkshire' and acknowledges Fielding as the painter (Fielden Pinxt) and Burgess as the draughtsman and

Figure 2. 'A North-West View of Halifax'. Engraving 1789, by William Burgess of Fielding original.

engraver (W. Burgess *del. et sculp.*) Though this appeared to differ in a few small details, there seemed no reason to doubt that the painting was the inspiration for the engraving, and that the engraver, William Burgess, had exercised a degree of artistic licence. Ling Roth also gives us a firm provenance, citing Whiteley Ward's grandfather as owner of the original painting.

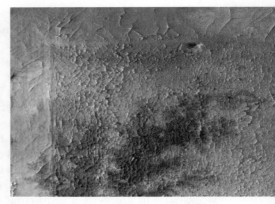

Figure 3. Detail of 'View of Halifax' prior to restoration.

The details of the picture were soon to disappear beneath a protective covering of tissue applied to the surface of the painting by the conservator and it remained thus for over ten years, until resources became available for a full restoration. When restoration was undertaken in 1993, a full examination of the paint pointed to 'extensive flaking and severe cupping - the paint layer being very brittle throughout, and a very poor adhesion of the paint layer to the support (the canvas)...the whole surface covered with a discoloured and yellowed varnish layer' (Figure 3). The eighteenth century canvas had not been relined, and no traces of a signature or any inscriptions appeared within the painting or on the back of the canvas. The painting was returned to Bankfield in its positive glory with its mellow blue and green hues. Once again the charm and grace of the painting was apparent. Nathan Fielding's original 'View of Halifax' had come home, or so we thought.

Then, as a bolt out of the blue, a London dealer offered the museum a variant version of 'Halifax from Haley Hill', of similar size yet with a trompe l'oeil frame (a simulated frame painted directly on the canvas). Details supplied stated that this painting was signed and dated 1768. It appeared to vary in a few small details, but fundamentally was the same as the Bankfield version.

We found ourselves unable to pursue this offer, as firstly the price far exceeded our resources, and secondly we felt we held the original. In this assumption we were mistaken. We might have understood this had we examined the differences more closely. As in all things, the devil is in the detail.

The enigmatic nature of the Bankfield painting is echoed in our

Figure 4. Nathan Fielding: Self-portrait 1797.
Courtesy Sothebys, London

somewhat slender knowledge of the life and work of Nathan Fielding. Historians have tended to relegate Nathan to footnotes to the life of his acclaimed son Anthony Van Dyck Copley Fielding (1787-1855), who became President of the Old Watercolour Society. Nathan Theodore Fielding will probably always be a somewhat shadowy figure of whom little is known and about whom little may be found. Dictionaries until recently were unable even to suggest a date of birth. The rediscovery of Nathan's self-portrait with its inscription 'Self-1797 Act 50' (Figure 4) permitted Waterhouse[2] to posit the year 1747 as his year of birth. Examination of the IGI records brings us, I believe, closer to the truth. They record that one Nathan Fielden was born on 6 July 1746 in the Parish of Ripponden, and that his father was Ely Fielding. The index also records a son of the same name born nine years earlier. One has to assume that this Nathan died in early childhood. It is interesting to note that a further Nathan Fielding was born in July 1753 in the same parish to a father with the same name. An understandable misreading of the IGI records led John Ramm[3] to suggest the date and place of birth of our painter as 1755 in Rochdale.

Enough of establishing Nathan's birth and claiming him as Calderdale's own son. What else we know of him is the evidence of his surviving paintings, the records of the birth of his siblings and a solitary eyewitness report. In 1804, a relation of Nathan's wife, a Reverend Mr Barker, visited the artist and his family in Keswick, and set down the following account.[4]

In the summer of 1804, the father of Copley Fielding was a lively, active man, of easy access and agreeable conversation, daily at the easel, painting 'con amore'. He showed his pictures readily, and not without much satisfaction. Of a head of an old man, which he had recently painted, and which had elicited some admiration, he said, 'Yes, they call me the English Denner'. He painted in oil, exclusively I think, and appeared as fond of landscape as of old faces. In his room were several small pictures, chiefly landscapes painted by him and copied by his sons. Taking up one, he said, 'Copley, is this mine or yours?' adding, 'We copy each other so exactly, it is difficult to know

which is which.' One day, on going in I found Mr Fielding finishing a
small picture in oils of Keswick Lake. In the sky was a light cloud
elaborately painted, and principal in effect. He joined in my
admiration of it and said, pointing to the cloud, 'it would take a touch
brighter,' and after a pause, 'No, I don't know.' My recollection of this
picture is that it was laboured in touch throughout, of a uniform
warmish green colour, and wanted aerial hues, and consequently space
and distance. Of another small picture he showed me - of a bluish hue,
he said, 'I was determined to see what ultramarine would do.' In colour
it reminded me a little of Paul Brill, or Velvet Breughel.

We have in Barker's account various points of interest when considering Bankfield's 'View of Halifax' - the emphasis on 'bluish' and green
hues, the laboured nature of the paint, and most importantly the fact
that his works were copied by his son and were indistinguishable as
such.

It appears that Fielding and his family settled in Keswick for only
a brief period. After leaving the Calder Valley this was to be the
pattern of their existence. Nathan was one of a substantial band of
itinerant painters, who plied their trade as painters of portraits,
topographical and picturesque landscapes. Unable to secure a
foothold in London, these artists were forced to move around the
smaller provincial centres, being prepared to undertake any suitable
work that came their way. These artists would tackle decorative
painting within houses, painting theatre scenery, heraldic and sign
painting, and even the copying and restoring of pictures. Nathan's
friend in Keswick, the Leeds-born artist Julius Caesar Ibbetson, talks
in his autobiography[5] of undertaking all these allied crafts. Sadly,
Nathan left no such record. However, his surviving works display a
substantial range of art practices: portraiture, miniature painting,
topographical landscapes, picturesque landscapes, watercolours,
etchings and aquatints. Hugely important was his role as teacher of
his six children, all of whom were to be artists in either a professional
or amateur capacity.

Nathan's travels appear to have begun shortly after the birth of his
third son Copley and when he had just turned forty. A number of his
sojourns are recorded by baptismal records, his paintings and
exhibition listings: Acton, on the fringes of London (1788),
Stamford, Lincolnshire (1793), Durham (1795-99) London (1800),
The Lake District, Ambleside and Keswick (1804), Manchester
(1806), Liverpool (1807-9) and London (1809-14).

But what of his first forty years, the years spent in the Calder

Figure 5. 'An Evening View of Field House', 1781. *(Courtesy Sotherbys, London)*

Valley? Our information remains slender: a marriage, the births of three children and a handful of known works. Nathan's earliest recorded work is a 'Dog's Head (in Chalk)', exhibited at the Free Society (in 1776) held at Mr Leignes', Northumberland Street, London. A watercolour dated 1777 appeared for sale at Chester in 1991, depicting 'Farm Labourers outside an Inn'.

The records of St Chad's, Rochdale, tell us that Nathan Theodore Fielding married Betty Barker on the 16 March 1780. Nathan was 33 and his bride some eight years his junior. The couple returned to East Sowerby and a year later in February 1781 their eldest son was born, and christened Theodore Henry Adolphus Fielding. 1781 also saw the completion of his earliest recorded large topographical painting, 'An Evening View of Field House and places adjacent from a Southern Eminence'. (Figure 5)[6] This and its companion completed the following year, 'A View of Rough Hey Wood and Lands Adjacent', were commissioned by George Stansfield for his mansion,

Figure 6. 'A View of Rough Hey Wood', 1782. *(Courtesy Sotherbys, London)*

Field House, in Sowerby (Figure 6). The first of these naturally focuses on the house, which in spite of being diminutive in relation to its surroundings, is placed dead centre. The house is surrounded by well-tended fields, some of which are given over to tenter frames with cloth stretched on them. Amongst the fields are fine warehouses, barns and well-kept roads. The painting is a celebration of ownership and prosperity. George Stansfield had inherited the estate from his grandfather in 1743, and immediately set about building a new house in the fashionable neo-classical idiom alongside the old hall, which had been erected some hundred years earlier. Prominent on the horizon is St Peter's Church, completed in 1763 with a substantial contribution from George Stansfield.

Both this painting and its companion show an artist of certain accomplishment, but still struggling against a distinct naivety. Both are suffused in a bluish tonality, which we are to witness again in the 'View of Halifax'. This was a feature of contemporary watercolours, due to the limitations of available pigments. One may reasonably assume that to have arrived at this level of accomplishment, Nathan must have undertaken some training, and that this most likely was with an art teacher in the Yorkshire region. One such was William

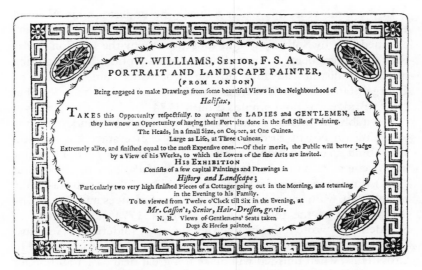

Figure 7. William Williams: advertising card, c.1792. *(Calderdale Museums)*

Williams, who in his later years took the young John Horner under his wing, engaging him to produce wool bale labels. Williams is another somewhat elusive figure; an itinerant artist recorded in Manchester (1763), Norwich (1768-70), York (1770-79), Shrewsbury (1780), Bath (1785-9) and London.[7] In 1775 he undertook the engravings for Reverend John Watson's *History of Halifax* with a 'View of Halifax' from the South East - the earliest recorded panoramic view of the town. An advertising card, issued by Williams around 1792,[8] talks of him 'being engaged to make drawings from some beautiful views in the neighbourhood of Halifax, and that these may be viewed at 'Mr Casson's, Senior, Hair-dresser'. The card (Figure 7) is a substantial puff for the artist, who styles himself 'W. Williams, Senior F.S.A. (Fellow of the Society of Arts) Portrait and Landscape Painter from London'. It continues by advertising his wares: 'Heads in a small size, on copper (miniatures) at one guinea. Large as Life, at three guineas...Paintings and Drawings in History and Landscape, particularly two very high finished Pieces of a Cottager going out in the morning, and returning in the evening to his family'. If all this sounds a touch familiar, then perhaps we have tracked down our quarry.

In 1784 a second son was born to Nathan and his wife, who now chose to call herself Elizabeth (no longer Betty). This was Frederick Felix Ferdinand Raphael Fielding.

In the same year, this writer believes, he undertook his 'View of Halifax from Haley Hill' with its trompe l'oeil frame, the date ascribed to it by Sotheby's,[9] and subsequently by the London dealer Richard Green, being a misreading of the inscription.[10] This painting displays a distinct advance on the two works commissioned by George Stansfield (1781-82), and perhaps one should mention that North Bridge was not completed until 1774.

Inevitably in this and the Bankfield version we find ourselves focussing on North Bridge, which takes centre stage - a graceful stone-built structure with six arches. It was built as part of a major improvement initiative instigated by Acts of Parliament (1740 and 1751) which encouraged what today would be called a private-public partnership. Money was raised by a group of trustees and secured by the promise of the toll levies. In October 1771 James Lister of Shibden Hall wrote to his brother Jeremy, then soldering in America: 'They are building a large bridge opposite Mr Dickenson's house to Cross Hills, when finished will make it a great deal easier and better getting to Halifax than ever the old one.' Building is said to have begun in the Spring of 1772 by Matthew Oates & Son of Northowram, using millstone grit quarried nearby. Four hundred feet in length and 28$^{1}/_{2}$ feet wide, it rose 56 feet above the bed of the Hebblebrook. When opened in the autumn of 1774 it was described as a 'massive and noble structure', and a toll bar was erected at the north end to provide for the debt repayments and for repairs. By the late 1860s this once noble structure was described as having 'blackened masonry and clumsy arches' and as 'a monument of the past'. It was replaced in the years following by Fraser's cast-iron bridge.[11]

A visiting clergyman, Thomas Twining, described Halifax in 1781 as 'in a bottom with monstrous hills about it. The Town is nothing extraordinary, except for the many magnificent houses lately built, and now daily building'. Thirteen years on, Rennie, Brown and Shirreff's report stated 'the houses are in general built of brick, though free-stone appears to abound in the neighbourhood'. John Horner's street views of Halifax, published in 1835, substantiate this. He was of course recording the situation prior to their massive clearance and the rebuilding programmes of the mid- and late nineteenth century. Today, brick buildings of the eighteenth century appear almost as an intrusion. This can be certainly said of the original Square Congregational Chapel built in 1772 and the wings of the substantial Georgian house at Wards End, built 1760-64.

Fielding's view gives emphasis to the 'monstrous hills', and substantiates Daniel Defoe's description of Halifax as

> *being so surrounded with hills, and those so high as makes the coming in and going out of it exceeding troublesome, and indeed for carriages hardly practicable, and particularly the hill which they go up to come out of the town eastwards towards Leeds, and which the country people call Halifax Bank, is so steep, so rugged, and sometimes too so slippery, that, to a town of so much business as this is, 'tis exceeding troublesome and dangerous.* [12]

Halifax Bank (also known as Old Bank and Beacon Hill) towers 400 feet above the town centre. It provides a natural divide between the millstone grit of the Calder Valley, and the coal-bearing shale of the Shibden Valley. At the time of Fielding's painting, coal was being mined from the shallow seams that criss-crossed the valley.

In the first version of the view, Halifax Bank appears to be covered in rough scrubland bordered by trees and bushes, which separate this land from the pattern of fields that surround the town. The engraving by Burgess displays a distinct enclosure on two-thirds of the hill, with the suggestion of what may well be quarrying within the enclosure. By the time Bankfield's version was painted this stony blemish is still apparent, albeit faintly, and rests outside a new line that traverses the hill separating scrubland from a plantation of trees that now covers half the hillside. We clearly see in the three versions the passage of time.

There are other indicators to time passing, for instance the ageing of the tree within the garden of the Mount on Haley Hill. Most tellingly, however, it is to be witnessed in the changes of fashion. If one were so inclined, one might almost view these figures as the evolution of a romantic tale. In the first we view a solitary gentleman admiring the flowering bush climbing the wall with his right hand touching gently one of the flowers. In the engraving his attention is turned to admiration of the young lady alongside him, and in the final version, whilst the lady gazes at him, his attention is on the young boy who appears to be plucking one of the flowers.

The inclusion of contemporary costumed figures is often a tell-tale indicator to the age of a painting. In the case of the earlier view we have a gentleman in fashionable attire of the early 1780s. He is wearing a lilac-coloured tailcoat with turned-down collar and pockets; the sheen on which suggests silk. Beneath this he has a white waistcoat, black breeches to just below the knee and white stockings. On his head he wears a black tricorn hat and in his left hand he carries a malacca cane. His escort in the engraving displays a gown with jacket typical of this period. Had the painting and print been produced in the 1760s or 70s we would have seen her in a hooped dress. The hoop has given way to the back bustle. The jacket has wide flounced lapels and short sleeves, and on her head she wears a mobcap.

We move forward into a different era in the Bankfield picture. The gentleman displays an entirely new colour sense, with his yellow breeches, and a rich brown cut-away frock coat with a black velvet collar. Both he and his young son are sporting black top hats. His wife, as we must assume it is, is dressed in the height of fashion with a single 'petticoat' of a white light material, which is girded beneath her breasts with a pink ribbon, creating a high waistline. This style took its inspiration from Greek drapery and line. Her bonnet is a similar material and appears to be surmounted by a single ostrich feather. In her right hand she holds the shaft of a parasol. All these fashion minutiae point to a date in the first few years after 1800. The Bankfield painting also points up one other costume detail. The second rider on the bridge is in military attire of a pattern that post-dates 1790.

On the far right of both paintings we can make out the row of 'full grown plane trees'[13] that defined the boundary of the lands belonging to Northgate House; moreover, there were no buildings between Northgate Chapel, Mr Lister's House (Northgate House) and Crosshills.[14] This is borne out in the first painting. However, by the time the second version was painted a new mansion with attached warehouse makes its appearance on the corner of what was to become North Parade. We know this to have been owned and occupied subsequently by Jonathan Akroyd. The mansion and the plane trees feature in a watercolour by John Horner, inscribed in his own hand 'Top of Winding Road 1810'. (Figure 8)[15]

So where does all this bring us? There can be no doubting the authenticity of the earlier signed painting. Bankfield's version continues as an enigma. If by Nathan Fielding, why was it not signed? I believe there was no need for a signature as the work was directly commissioned from the artist. However, it is also my belief that the work was actually undertaken as a collaborative venture by the Fielding family and that the landscape was substantially laid down by Nathan's third son, Copley, whilst the sky was painted by his eldest son, Theodore.

But when was this? I would suggest the year 1805. Clearly the costume details and the mansion on Northgate bring us close to this date. However, perhaps (and it is only perhaps) a significant indicator

Figure 8. John Horner; 'Top of Winding Road', 1810. *(Calderdale Museums)*

is the long red, white and blue textile tentered in the fields. This is
tantalisingly placed dead centre, and just in front of the Parish
Church. Might this have been placed there as part of the celebrations
of Nelson's success at the Battle of Trafalgar?

In 1805, we understand the Fielding family was once again on the
move, from the Lakes down to Manchester, following the death of
Elizabeth. Theodore would have been 24 and Copley 18. Copley, as
we know from Barker's account, was already a faithful copyist. The
evidence that Theodore may have tackled the sky comes from a small
painting of a 'Mountain River'.[15] This displays not only a similar
pattern of brush strokes, but more importantly the same cracklelure
that led to the fugitive nature of the sky in the Bankfield work.

Our elusive painter disappeared around 1814; his last known
address was 4 Bridgewater Street, Somer's Town, East London, and
one of his last exhibited works was 'The Botanist with a Nondescript
Fern'. This, of course, points to a significant part of Nathan's output,
his portraiture, which has only been alluded to here. Where now is

his 'Portrait of Elias Hoyle of Sowerby aged 113', painted in 1793? Would it be signed? Would we recognise it if we saw it? The lesson of all this has to be never to accept things on face value, and always to look closer and analyse the evidence with ever-greater care in order to suggest an attribution.

Notes and References

1. Roth, Henry Ling. 'Fielding's Painting of Halifax'. *Halifax Naturalist Vol VI No 31*, April 1901 pp 1-3. Revised version published in Ling Roth, *The Yorkshire Coiners*.
2. Waterhouse, Ellis. *Dictionary of British Eighteenth-Century Painters*, London 1981.
3. Ramm, John. 'In Search of Nature - Anthony Vandyke Copley Fielding', *Antique Dealer and Collectors' Guide*, May 1999, pp 28-31.
4. Quoted in full: Roget, John Lewis. *A History of the Old Watercolour Society - Vol 1*, London 1891, pp 258.
5. Ibbetson, Julius Caesar. *An Accidence or Gamut of Painting in Oils and Watercolours, 1803.*
6. Two oil paintings on canvas each 561/2 in x 681/2 in (143.5 cm x 174.5 cm). With the family until sold at Sotheby's 13 July 1988 (Lots 66 and 67).
7. Waterhouse 1981, p 412.
8. Bankfield Museum. Inserted within an album assembled by John and Joshua Horner. John Horner' (1787-1867) is best known for his twenty lithographs, *Buildings in the Town and Parish of Halifax*, published 1835.
9. Sold at Sotheby's 18 November 1988 (Lot 60) as 'A prospect of a town, probably in Yorkshire, with mills and a viaduct, and figures in the foreground'.
10. It is possible that Nathan was dyslexic, for he signed one of his later works 'Nathan Fieling': 'View of Stamford, Lincolnshire' (Peterborough Art Gallery).
11. For a full description and history of the North Bridges see Douglas Taylor and Harry Armitage, 'North Bridges', *Transactions of the Halifax Antiquarian Society* (THAS) 1969.
12. Daniel Defoe. *A Tour through the Whole Island of Great Britain,* 1724-6.
13. As described in the so-called *Itinerary of Halifax* and quoted in John Williams, 'Northgate House, Halifax', *THAS* 1959.
14. 1775, as remembered by Thomas Sutcliffe of Ovenden Hall, *THAS* 1955.
15. 'A Mountain River', illustrated in *The Old English Landscape Painters Vol IV*, Col. M H Grant, F Lewis, Leigh-on-Sea, 1959.

4. Hearts, Circles, Diamonds and Scrolls: External Decoration on Seventeenth Century Houses

by David Cant

ONE OF THE REMARKABLE CHARACTERISTICS of the upper Calder valley is the survival of a relatively large number of stone houses built over 300 years ago. Constructed of local materials, some also display unusual external decoration.

This article deals with one of the decorative features, the hoodmould terminal. The hoodmould is a projecting course of stone along the outside of a building. It may be continuous, stepping up or down over window and door openings, or confined to the area just above those openings. In many cases in the upper Calder valley the hoodmould ends in a decorated feature called a 'terminal' or 'stop'.

The Background

The parish of Halifax in 1600 covered about 140 square miles. It stretched from the old boundary with Lancashire, at Todmorden, in the west, to Brighouse in the east. The prosperity of this area, based predominantly on the expanding textile industry, grew significantly from the mid-sixteenth century.[1] One consequence was that local families had the means to improve the places where they lived and worked. They rebuilt their existing timber-framed house or constructed new buildings of stone.

The stone used was either millstone grit, which predominates to the west of Halifax, or the thinner flagstone. The gritstone in particular is a tough durable material which naturally weathers to a dark grey colour. It was, however, relatively easy to work when 'green', that is, recently quarried. The local masons took advantage of this feature to decorate the houses they built with copings supported by shaped stones known as kneelers, finials above the apex of the gables and on other roof surfaces, decorated porches and door surrounds, and with courses of projecting stonework, particularly over doors and windows.

This projecting course of stonework has been called by various names. The terms dripstone and dripmould were used by some nineteenth and twentieth century architectural writers. It seems to

Figure 1. Old Hall, Norland, demolished in 1914 for export to America!
Halifax Antiquarian Society

imply that the stone would give some kind of protection from water running down the building. I prefer hoodmould, a term 'still in use in Yorkshire' in the nineteenth century.[2] This implies that it may be the term used by the masons themselves, although no word has been identified from the few surviving building accounts of the period.[3]

Although hoodmoulds are a common feature of stone and brick buildings in most parts of the country, the use of decorated terminals is less common. Isolated examples can be found in most places where stone is the local building material. However, the area covered by the old parish of Halifax is noted for the frequency with which they occur. Neighbouring areas of Yorkshire and Lancashire do have examples, but in nothing like the numbers which have survived in the upper Calder valley (Figure 1).

One hundred and twenty houses have (or had, as some have been demolished) decorated hoodmould terminals (Figure 2). They occurred on a significant number of houses in the old townships of

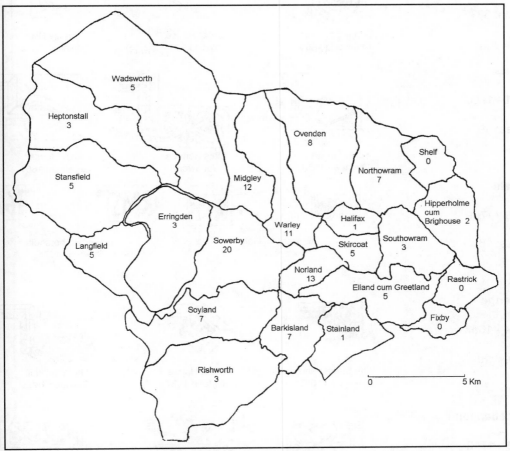

Figure 2. Houses with hoodmould terminals in the townships of the Parish of Halifax. *D Cant*

Sowerby (20), Norland (13), Midgley (12) and Warley (11), and in most of the other townships of the parish. Decorated terminals were also used in seventeenth century alterations to churches, indeed some survive from the dormers of the old church at Heptonstall.

The Designs

At first glance there seems to be an endless variety of designs for these terminals. Nevertheless, there are a number of common forms used as a basis for most of them (Figure 3). They are:

- a circle, sometimes formed into a spiral or filled with a face (Figure 4)

Circles

1607 - 1706

Styles: 33

Upper Cockcroft
Rishworth 1607

Great House
Soyland 1624

Castle Hill
Sowerby 1662

Hearts

1601 - 1706

Styles: 39

Lee House
Ovenden 1625

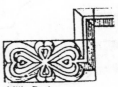

Little Burlees
Wadsworth

Clay House
Greetland 1661

Initials

1628 - 1709

Styles: 16

Lower Old Hall
Norland 1634

Lower Hathershelf
Sowerby 1671

Lozenge

1614 - 1662

Styles: 19

High Sunderland
Northowram 1620s

Great House
Soyland 1624

Ovenden Hall
Ovenden 1662

Miscellaneous

1615 - 1712

Styles: 16

Barkisland Hall
Barkisland 1638

Lower Spark House
Norland 1677

Greenwood Lee
Heptonstall 1712

Scrolls

1605 - 1691

Styles: 28

Fields
Norland 1616

Howroyd
Barkisland 1642

Norland Hall
Norland 1672

Figure 3. Terminal designs in Calderdale. *D Cant*

- a heart, usually on its side (Figure 5)
- a lozenge or diamond (Figure 6)
- a scroll, frequently used in pairs or fours to form other shapes

Some of the more elaborate terminals use a combination of these designs. Fallingworth Hall and Lower Old Hall in Norland both have various combinations. Inevitably, some designs do not fall into any of these categories. These have been grouped together under the miscellaneous heading.

There is a further group, in which the terminals are formed by the initials of the person for whom the work was done, sometimes accompanied by the date. *The Lord Nelson* in Luddenden has the initials of Gregory Patchett in the terminals on the first floor. The date 1634 and his initials are also carved on the door lintel. The top storey window of the central gable of Barkisland Hall has the initials JG for John Gledhill and '16' on the left, and '38' and SG for his wife Sarah on the right. They were making a clear statement in stone about their status and ability to afford such a grand building.

It is quite common to find the design reversed at the other end of the window, as at Mytholmroyd Farm. Most houses only have one or two basic designs. Out of the 120 houses, over 80 fall into this category. A select few boast five or six designs, for example Barkisland Hall, Wood Lane Hall

Figure 4. Little Burlees, Wadsworth. *D Cant*

Figure 5. South Clough Head, Warley. *A Sinclair*

Figure 6. Little Burlees, Wadsworth. *D Cant*

and Little Burlees (Figures 4, 6, 9,). A repeated pattern, such as the hearts over the upper floor windows at Clay House, West Vale, is an exception.

The illustrations show something of the variety of each basic design type (Figure 3). The circle and heart shapes have the most variety. They are also the most common designs found. On some buildings, one basic design shape is formed by combining others, for example using scrolls to form the outline of a heart, as at The Howroyd. Other elaborate terminals have been created by combining different designs. A lozenge and heart have been incorporated in one design, together with two little hearts, at Long Can, Ovenden, a house with a particularly rich collection of terminals (Figure 5, 7 & 8).

A few terminals actually bear a date, but most have to be given an approximate date by looking at other stonework on the house which is associated with the same period of building. For example, door lintels may be dated, sometimes with initials which help to identify the person for whom the work was done. In some cases it is possible to identify a building and its occupants from documentary sources. Of the 120 houses with decorated terminals, 50 do not have a specific date. However, the style and layout of the buildings make it unlikely that they will fall far outside the ranges given.

Figure 7. Long Can, Ovenden. *D Cant*

Where it has been possible to assign a date, a number of observations can be made about the designs. In general, it seems that the simpler designs were earlier, with the more complex and elaborate designs coming after 1630. The stone houses of the late sixteenth and early seventeenth century tend to have less external decoration than those built in the middle and towards the end of the seventeenth century. This is probably linked with fashionable

Figure 8. Long Can, Ovenden. *D Cant*

trends and the skills of the local masons. One local house with substantial external decoration was High Sunderland, believed to have been rebuilt for the wealthy Sunderland family in 1629. Although it was demolished in 1950, photographs show small lozenge shapes on the hoodmould terminals. During the 1630s houses like Long Can and Barkisland Hall, although not so elaborate, illustrated a growing trend of external decoration.

On many houses, only certain windows have decorated terminals over them. In general, such decoration was applied to the prominent elevation of the house, particularly where it would be visible from the access road or trackway. This suggests that the decoration was as much for the benefit of other people as for those who actually lived in the house. Decorative terminals are more usual on the upper floor 'chamber', and the ground floor 'parlour' and 'housebody', the main living room. They are seldom found over workshop windows, except as part of a continuous hoodmould covering the whole front elevation.[4]

Symbolic Significance
Decorated hoodmould terminals can be seen on mediaeval church

Figure 9. Decoration at Little Burlees, Wadsworth. *D Cant*

buildings, often in the form of a head, foliage or a shield, and on a few secular stone buildings. It is not certain where the craftsmen found their inspiration for the local designs in the seventeenth century. Many of these designs are also on furniture of the period; for example, the lozenge is a typical feature of north-country wooden chair backs. Hearts and scrolls were carved on large cupboards and dressers. Textile patterns also incorporate some of the designs found on the buildings. Studies of motifs suggest that many such designs have existed for a long time, having been transferred from culture to culture.

Did the designs have a particular symbolic meaning for the people of the seventeenth century? Certain links can be made with known symbolic references, and where these were well-known and accepted we could assume their use was intentional, for example, the heart used as a symbol of love, understanding and compassion.[5] However, Ambler described some of these shapes as 'devils-arrows', more associated with power, virility and perhaps protection from harm.[6]

Research has been underway for some years into protective and ritual marks on and in buildings, such as on heck or hex posts or over openings.[7] Other traditions, such as hiding artefacts in wall cavities or recesses, show these had definite significance for those who followed them. The lozenge is just one of a number of symbols of fertility. The continuation of the family name through male descendants was very important in the seventeenth century.

The depiction of a head with a face on some terminals may be linked to the wider practice of carving heads over doorways or gateways (Figure 4). A number of suggestions have been made for their interpretation – the portrayal of the owner; a link to royalty (particularly ironic as Charles I lost his head in 1649); a protective device for the building and occupants. Heads in particular have been studied in some detail.[8] A nineteenth-century stonemason, John Castillo, described the 'aud man's face' he was carving. This may well be a link to the protective power of the image.[9]

The Craftsmen
It is clear from the surviving buildings that a number of skilled masons, their labourers and apprentices were working in the area throughout the seventeenth century. On most buildings the master mason would have been responsible for implementing the wishes of the client, co-ordinating the overall design and the other craftsmen. From the rare surviving building accounts, it is possible to get an idea of their methods of work and payment.

Local masons have been identified from the Akroyd and Bentley families. They were working on Bradley Hall, Stainland, and Heath Grammar School, Halifax, at the end of the sixteenth century. They were employed subsequently by the Savile family on their houses at Methley and Howley. In the early seventeenth century they did work on some Oxford colleges.[10] Some returned to continue working around Halifax, and they may have brought back the idea of applying decorated features such as the hoodmould terminals to local houses. Further research may establish links between them and other local buildings.

Less is known about their working practices. It is likely, given the difficulties of transporting heavy material, that the stone was quarried near the site where it was to be used. Rough dressing may have taken place at the quarry, with more detailed ornamental work such as the terminals being carved at the 'lodge' on site. If there were templates for the designs, they were probably used for the basic shapes, with the detail being carved freehand. This would explain the large number of detail differences found.

It seems clear from the continuity and range of dates that at least three generations of masons were carving decorated terminals. It is known that two generations of the Akroyd family were masons, and continuity between generations is likely in other families. Less directly the skills would have been passed to apprentices who in turn became masters and trained others.

The Houses
The different types of houses have been described in studies such as the thesis by Christopher Stell, which has a section on decorated terminals.[11] Books such as *Rural Houses of West Yorkshire*, and the pioneering study by Louis Ambler, also mention them. To assess their significance it is necessary to estimate the number of seventeenth-century houses and the proportion that were decorated with hoodmould terminals.

The population of the Parish of Halifax has been estimated to have been between 18,000 to 20,000 around the middle of the seventeenth century.[12] If the average household size was around five persons, this suggests around 4,000 dwellings. A substantial proportion of these would have been the homes of artisans, tradespeople, those who worked for others in the textile trades, labourers and farm workers. Few of their houses have survived, particularly in towns such as Halifax, where progressive renewal of the buildings is recorded in documents from the eighteenth century.

The buildings that have survived are likely to be the larger ones, in locations where there was less economic pressure for their replacement. North of Halifax, for example, there are only scattered survivors amongst nineteenth and twentieth century development. In contrast, the hillsides of the upper Calder valley and its tributaries have many substantial buildings of the seventeenth century. Only a small proportion of these houses have external decoration such as decorated terminals. These are likely to be the homes of the more prosperous inhabitants in the seventeenth century.

By the beginning of the twentieth century many of the older houses had been divided into a number of dwellings, in response to the accommodation needs of the expanding population in the nineteenth century. New doorways had been broken through, mullions removed from the windows, and guttering and pipes fixed to the buildings. Often this work was done with little regard for the look of the building or the decorative features. When such a building fell into disrepair, such as Binn Royd, Norland, or became unstable after being struck by lightning, like Norland Hall, the solution adopted was to demolish it (Figure 1).

It is fortunate that local historians have taken an interest in these older buildings. There are good photographs of many that have now disappeared, or been subsequently rebuilt. These photographs and drawings have contributed to our knowledge and provided evidence that would otherwise be lost. The records of members of the Halifax Antiquarian Society, particularly H P Kendall, have proved invaluable in widening the scope of this survey.[13] By identifying some of the people for whom the decorative work was done it may be possible to explain the occurrence of so many decorated terminals.

The Families

None of the major gentry families of the West Riding lived in the parish of Halifax in the seventeenth century. There were, however, a number of minor gentry families, who, together with wealthy yeoman, making their money principally by acting as merchants or middlemen in the expanding textile industry, were responsible for building many of the houses which survive today.[14]

It is worth considering their social background, their political and religious beliefs, their desires and aspirations, to see if there are any links between these aspects and the decoration on the houses. It is difficult to see things through their eyes, particularly as the limited surviving documentary evidence includes few contemporary accounts, and there is little to explain why certain people had carved decorations on their hoodmould terminals while others had none.

It is possible to identify some of the families who had the work done either from physical evidence such as initials carved on the house, or from documentary sources. Using the latter probably leads to a concentration on families with higher status, who were probably the wealthier ones, as their records are more likely to have survived. Despite this drawback the surviving evidence on the houses themselves permits a number of observations to be made.

In addition, several families who would have described themselves as yeomen at the end of the sixteenth century, acquired minor gentry status within two or three generations. The Dearden family of Sowerby are typical of this improved status. Richard, who was Constable of Sowerby in 1609, purchased a property known as Wood Lane in 1615. His son John (1617-83) rebuilt the house in 1649 in good quality stonework. There is an elegant two-storey porch and a wealth of decorative detail, including a variety of hoodmould terminals.[15] Indeed, the ability to build such a house was probably one of the prerequisites for attaining higher status, particularly in the eyes of the established minor gentry.

There are other families, however, who did not become part of the gentry. Although they generated considerable wealth through their business activities, and built substantial stone houses, they continued to describe themselves as 'yeoman'. The Taylor family of Norland is a good example of this group.[16] Their prosperity was expressed in Lower Old Hall, of 1634, Norland Hall, rebuilt in 1672 but demolished in 1912, and Upper Hall, of 1690. These are all large houses for the area, with good quality stonework and many decorative features. The Taylors were probably typical of a larger number of families than the Deardens. They continued to play an important part in local affairs into the eighteenth century.

In trying to untangle the complex political and religious associations of local families, one is left with the impression that some regarded events such as the civil war and the nonconformist difficulties in the 1660s and 1670s as annoying interruptions to the more important business of working, trading and ensuring one's family continued to live in the style to which they were accustomed. There does seem to be a reduction in housebuilding around the unsettled period during the early phase of the civil war in Yorkshire from 1642 to the occupation of the Halifax area by Royalist troops from July 1643 to January 1644. But outside this period and the subsequent protectorship, there seem to be just as much construction, from the evidence of dated buildings.

A few local families were active supporters of the Royalist cause. Richard Gledhill of Barkisland Hall was killed at the battle of Marston Moor; the Sunderlands were eventually forced to dispose of their showpiece house at High Sunderland because of their involvement on the losing side. Both these families had houses with a significant amount of external decoration. Other families actively supported the Parliamentarians, such as Joseph Fourness of Ovenden Hall, who served on the Payment to Parliamentary Soldiers Committee of 1646. His house also has decorated terminals, although more restrained than High Sunderland or Barkisland Hall. Many other local families supported the parliamentary cause, and some of their houses have decorated hoodmould terminals. Political belief does not seem to have affected choice.

The strong nonconformist tradition which developed in the parish of Halifax throughout the seventeenth century had clear links to the ethics of hard work and self-determination. It might be expected that such people would not indulge in elaborate decoration of their houses. Perhaps this gives some clue as to the development of hoodmould terminals as a decorative art form in this area. They can hardly be described as flamboyant decoration, certainly in terms of some of the styles of post-restoration England, but they do give the opportunity for a muted display of prosperity without being ostentatious. The more elaborate designs develop in the middle of the century and particularly following the restoration of the monarchy in 1660.

Conclusion

The Halifax area had a proportionately large number of wealthy yeoman families compared to other parts of northern England and indeed the country. The layout and style of the houses that they built, and the decoration on them, reflected their ideas and achievements. In this context the hoodmould terminals and other decorated features become the outward display of successful families achieving recognition and status, at least in their own locality. We are fortunate that so many of these buildings have survived to be enjoyed today.

The fashion for decorated terminals seems to have died out at the beginning of the eighteenth century. The porch at Greenwood Lee, Heptonstall, of 1712 has a window with decorated terminals. It appears to be the end of an era. However, there was some 'vernacular revival' work in the late-nineteenth century to buildings like Ovenden Hall, which has a wing with decorated terminals complementing the seventeenth century one already there. In recent years local stonemasons have been carving these features again, in most cases to restore or complement work done some three to four hundred years before.

Notes and References

1 B Jennings, *Pennine Valley: A History of Upper Calderdale*. Smith Settle, Otley, 1992, chaps 6-8; M E Francois, 'The Social and Economic Development of Halifax 1558 - 1640', *Proceedings of the Leeds Philosophical and Literary Society* Vol XI, April 1966.
2 J H Parker, *Glossary of Terms used in Gothic Architecture*. Fifth Ed., Oxford 1850, p 186.
3 For published local building accounts: J Stead, 'Dr Henry Power and his alterations at New Hall Elland', *Old West Riding* Vol 8 No 2, Winter 1988; W B Trigg, 'Ovenden Houses', *Transactions of Halifax Antiquarian Society (THAS)* 1928 pp 353-4.
4 C Giles, *Rural Houses of West Yorkshire*. Royal Commission on Historic Monuments, HMSO, 1986; for position of these rooms in typical houses see Jennings, p 86.
5 J C Cooper, *Illustrated Encyclopaedia of Traditional Symbols*. Thames & Hudson, London, 1978.
6 L Ambler, *The Old Halls and Manor Houses of Yorkshire*. London, 1913, fig 50.
7 A Armstrong, 'Protective Markings in Yorkshire Buildings'. *Journal of Yorkshire Vernacular Buildings Study Group* 1998.
8 J Billingsley, *A Stony Gaze: Investigating Celtic and other stone heads*. Capall Bann, Chieveley, 1998.
9 P Brears, *North Country Folk Art*. John Donald, Glasgow, 1989, chap 3.
10 T W Hanson. 'Halifax Builders in Oxford' *THAS* 1928.

11 C F Stell, 'Vernacular Architecture in a Pennine Community'. Unpub. MA Thesis, University of Liverpool, 1960. Copy in Halifax Reference Library.

12 Francois, *op cit*, p 225.

13 H P Kendall's photographic collection at West Yorkshire Archives, Calderdale, articles in THAS, and in the Society's Library.

14 Francois, *op cit*, chap 2.

15 Giles, *op cit*, pp 57-62, 216; and H P Kendall, 'Famous Sowerby Mansions' *THAS*, 1906.

16 H P Kendall, 'Ancient Halls of Norland' *THAS*, 1904.

Acknowledgements

The survey of hoodmould terminals which forms the basis of this article has been compiled from photographic collections, illustrations and personal observation. I am particularly grateful to a members of the Halifax Antiquarian Society and the Yorkshire Vernacular Buildings Study Group for keeping me supplied with a steady flow of photographs and for discussion which has helped my understanding. I would welcome further information on decorated terminals from any part of the country.

Most of the houses mentioned are visible from a public road or footpath. Please respect the privacy of the occupants when looking at buildings.

5. JAMES ALDERSON, BREWERY PROPRIETOR

by Peter Robinson

MR JAMES ALDERSON OF LUDDENDEN, though of humble birth, was destined to become one of the leading figures in the brewing industry in Northowram and later Halifax.

Alderson began work at the age of ten years, and whilst a young man commenced business on his own account as a grocer at Claremount. Before many years had passed he turned his attention instead towards the brewing industry, which was undergoing rapid expansion during the middle years of the nineteenth century in response to urban population growth.[1] He entered into partnership with one James Shepherd, of whom nothing is known except that he resided in Horley Green Road, Claremount, and was presumably well known to Alderson either through friendship or business connection.

Lower Brear Brewery, Leeds Road, Stump Cross, Halifax

The business was established at Lower Brear, though it is unclear whether the brewery was already in existence when Shepherd & Alderson formed their partnership, for in 1866 Mr Thomas Howarth offered the tenancy of the *Old Dumb Mill Inn*, giving Lower Brear as his address.[2] Howarth is more generally associated with the operation of the Hipperholme Steam Brewery which had been in existence prior to 1851 and was located further along Leeds Road on land known as Tan House Field.[3] The site of Shepherd and Alderson's brewery is now occupied by Fletcher Brothers, car dealers, but was at that time owned by John Lister of Shibden Hall, from whom it was let. In April 1876 the partnership with Shepherd came to an end by mutual consent and the business was continued by Alderson on his own account.[4]

Soon the premises became too small for the scale of operations and substantial alterations were required. At the end of 1882 tenders were invited for the erection of new stables, the removal of the brewhouse roof, the raising of its walls and the construction of a new roof topped by a large ventilator. The following tenders were received by John Lister for the work to be carried out - it is not recorded who received the contract, but the summary sheet indicates that the combined tender of £68 10s 0d (£68.50) was favoured with plumbing work as extra.[5]

	Masons	Joiners	Slaters	Total
Joseph Hanson, Horley Green Wood Works, Claremount (Joinery only)		£20 16s 0d		£20 16s
W Ratcliffe & Sons, Claremount (Masonry/Joinery/Plumbing/Slating)	£89 0s 0d *			£89 0s
Ramsden & Slater (Masonry/Joinery/Slating)	£80 11s 0d			£80 11s
Thomas Cordingley, Chester Road, Akroydon (Masonry/Joinery/Plumbing/Slating)	£86 11s 0d *			£86 11s
Joseph & William Pickles (Masonry only)	£34 10s 0d			£34 10s
W Denton, Swan Bank, Halifax (Joinery only)		£25 0s 0d		
S Pickles & Sons, Great Northern Street, Halifax			£9 0s 0d	£68 10s
T Rushworth & Firth (Slating & Plastering)			£9 0s 0d	£9 0s

*   Includes plumbing work carried out by C A Walshaw of 53 Lister Lane, Halifax, of £1 15s 0d.

The drawings for the work were prepared for John Lister by Mr Proctor.[6]

The 1860s and 1870s had been a period of rapid urbanisation, and Alderson's Brewery was well placed to take advantage of the expanding markets in both Halifax and Bradford. Despite the increased levels of control which had come about in 1869 by the return of beerhouse licences within the jurisdiction of local licencing justices, it was nevertheless still possible to obtain new licences. Only a third of public houses and beerhouses in central Halifax were tied to breweries by 1876, with a lower proportion in outlying districts. In other areas of the West Riding woollen district this proportion was lower still; furthermore there was a steady flow of publicans relinquishing the brewing side of their businesses in order to concentrate on retailing alone. Alderson, along with other common brewers, continued to thrive, but with competition increasing it was clear that the only way to secure business in the future was through the acquisition of a tied estate of pubs and beerhouses. There is evidence that some local brewers used the loan tie as a means of securing business, as well as by the acquisition of short-term leases.[7] Nevertheless, the favoured method was outright purchase of property, which not only tied the business, but provided assets against which loans could be obtained in order to finance further acquisition. At the same time income in the form of rents was obtained from the non-licensed portions of any property acquired, over and above the 'dry' and 'wet' rents available from the publican.[8] Alderson had in fact purchased his first tied outlet, a beerhouse at Clayton near Bradford called *The Sportsman*, as early as July 1874. More than a decade then elapsed before the *Hen & Chickens* in Winding Road, Halifax, was acquired; thereafter additional outlets were obtained as opportunity and finances permitted. These included the *Victoria and Albert*, Haley Hill, Halifax (1887); the *Oddfellows*, Lidget Green (1895); and the *Rose and Crown*, Cote Hill, Halifax (1897).[9]

Park Brewery (later Windmill Hill Brewery), The Hough, Northowram

James Alderson, by now a successful and prosperous businessman, sought to establish better premises for his brewery as well as to provide himself with a suitable dwelling house appropriate to his new-found status. To this end he bought a plot of land at Mount Pleasant, west of the Halifax and Bradford Old Road near the top of the Hough in October 1896; the vendor, Frank Shepherd, may well have had connections with his former partner, James Shepherd. Early in the following year, Alderson also bought the adjacent Windmill Field.

To design his new house and brewery he chose an up-and-coming local architect, Joseph Frederick Walsh. Walsh had already worked on a new maltings for Halifax brewers, Richard Whitaker &

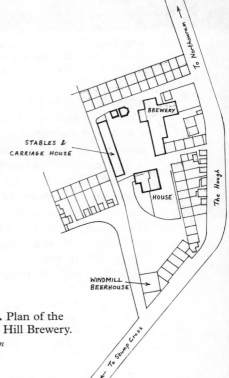

Figure 1. Plan of the Windmill Hill Brewery.
P W Robinson

Figure 2. The gatehouse to the former Windmill Hill Brewery in 1999. *P W Robinson*

Sons, had obtained commissions for the design of several Halifax Board Schools and was establishing for himself a reputation for the design of high-quality gentlemen's residences of distinction.[10] The brewery buildings themselves were ranged around a central courtyard, entrance to which was controlled by a two-storey, semi-octagonal office and gatehouse (Figure 2). The main brewery buildings comprised a brewery tower, tun room, cooler and loading bay. A large cast-iron tank surmounted the tower, into which the brewing liquor was pumped from a 90ft (27.4m) borehole. The brewery, upon completion, was initially named the Park Brewery, but soon after opening this was changed to the Windmill Hill Brewery. Facing it across the yard was a long, low range of buildings which housed the stables, harness room and carriage house. The house itself faced south, overlooking a steeply sloping garden, and was executed in a vernacular style of architecture. Pitch-faced stone was used for the wall stones with ashlar stone for the mullioned and transomed windows as well as the dressings and other decorative work; all supplied by the nearby Ringby quarries. The roof was covered with Buttermere slate and both oak and pine were extensively used for the interior. Heating for the building was provided by means of both open fires and a central heating system using American radiators. The water heating system was located beneath the wash-house and heat was also provided to the harness room and carriage room.[11] Above the main entrance to the house is a stone tablet decorated with the owner's initials, the date 1897 and various barley and hop motifs (Figure 3).

At the end of 1900 the

Figure 3. The carved tablet above the main door of Alderson's house. *P W Robinson*

business was converted to a limited liability company under the style of James Alderson & Co Ltd. This type of conversion was often undertaken by brewery businesses at this time as a way of enabling the proprietors to realise part of their capital invested in the business whilst retaining overall control. Additional funding for expansion could be obtained both from new investors in the business, and by the simplification of borrowing arrangements through the issue of debentures. The three initial directors were James Alderson, William Oates and Frank H Hatch.[12] Oates, who lived at Spring Head, Northowram, was a wealthy local businessman and co-owner of a large brick and tile manufacturing company based at Horley Green, whilst Hatch of Quarry House, Northowram, was Alderson's manager and head brewer, having previously operated on his own account at a brewery situated at Brackenbed, Mount Pellon. By the time of the Company's formation, two further houses had been added to the tied estate, namely the *Who Could a'Thowt It* at Southowram in 1898 and the *Bridge Tavern* in Brighouse during 1900.

Not a great deal is known about the beers produced by the company, although an advertisement of 1906 gives some clue as to its output.[13] The beers advertised are four different types of ale at 10d, 1s, 1s 2d and 1s 4d per gallon (4p, 5p, 6p and 7p) and a speciality Oatmeal Stout at 1s 2d (6p) per gallon. Comparison with the products of other local brewers at this time suggests that the cheapest types of ale would perhaps have been different strengths of mild, or a dark mild and a light bitter beer for family use. The 1s 2d beer would perhaps have been a best or light mild, the type of beer for which Halifax was best known, while that sold for 1s 4d was probably an old beer. In the case of Samuel Webster & Sons of the Fountain Head Brewery in Ovenden, their XXX Best Mild and Extra Stout each sold at 1s 2d per gallon in 1897.[14]

It should be borne in mind, however, that typical beer strengths were much higher than at present. Duty was collected on a 'standard barrel' of beer with an original gravity of 1055 degrees, which would have yielded a beer of perhaps 5 to 5.5 per cent alcohol by volume. The higher priced beers such as stouts would undoubtedly have been stronger still than this. Typically a pint of ordinary draught bitter today would be 3.5 to 4 per cent alcohol by volume.

As well as cask beers, Alderson also bottled a portion of their output using bottles supplied by Messrs. Kilner Brothers of Thornhill Lees, Dewsbury.[15]

By the end of the century Alderson was an old man and he

probably did not maintain a very active interest in the concern after the formation of the limited company. His wife had died in 1901, and since the couple had no children, he had gone to live with his nephew and niece, Mr and Mrs Walton. During 1908 he had purchased Undercliffe House where he then took up residence. His health had been in decline for some time and eventually he died, aged 76, at the end of October 1908. He was interred at St Thomas' Church, Claremount.[16]

During the last third of the nineteenth century brewers had enjoyed a buoyant market for their beers, but increased competition had gradually forced them to look towards public house acquisition as a means of securing business, such that by 1897 no less than 89 per cent of outlets in Halifax were owned by breweries.[17] A depressed textile trade was repeatedly cited in the 1890s for almost static profits, whilst the new century brought the return of a Liberal government unsympathetic to the beer and liquor trades. Their *Licensing Act* of 1904 established a statutory principle of public house closure on the grounds of non-necessity, and set up a compensation fund, contributions to which had to be provided by the brewers themselves. Between 1905 and 1914, a total of 41 licences were removed in Halifax Borough alone. With static sales and virtually all outlets owned by brewery companies, defensive mergers were seen as a way of maintaining profitability. Utilising finance provided by the Halifax and Huddersfield Union Bank, James Alderson & Co Ltd acquired the business of the Halifax Brewery Company based at Cote Hill near Halifax, together with 36 public houses, beer-houses, off licences and former licensed premises.[18]

Victoria Brewery, Cote Hill, Halifax

The origins of the Victoria Brewery (Figure 4) at Cote Hill, like Alderson's Lower Brear concern, date from the middle years of the nineteenth century. In May 1852 the sixteen-year unexpired portion of a lease on the Victoria brewery, together with a cottage, two-stalled stable and a close of land, was offered for sale in the *Halifax Guardian*. Also on offer was the stock in trade and brewery utensils, which comprised 40 casks of Best and Table beer, $3^{1}/_{2}$ pockets of hops, brewing pan, liquor pan, mashing troughs, coolers, working vats, piping, empty casks, cart, set of harness and other articles used in the trade.[19]

The purchaser was a local man, John Naylor, who energetically set about the expansion of his new business. As early as 1854 he began to establish a tied estate for himself, initially with leasehold acquisitions, and later with freehold purchases. In 1864 he had one of his most prestigious houses, a former coaching inn, the *Bull's Head* in Sowerby Bridge, almost completely rebuilt. The new hotel, designed by Messrs Hepworth and Helliwell, architects of Brighouse, included a spacious coffee room, dining room and cosy smoke room.[20] Aimed at both family and business patronage, it boasted excellent cuisine and a well-stocked wholesale wine department.[21]

Within a couple of years Hepworth and Helliwell were again called upon to prepare plans, this time for the erection of new brewery premises at Cote Hill, to be built on the latest tower principle. Within the top of the tower was a tank containing the brewing liquor, beneath which successive stages of the brewing process were located on separate

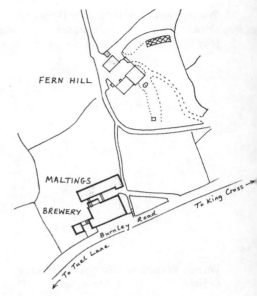

Figure 4. Plan of the Victoria Brewery. *P W Robinson*

floors. Eventually the finished beer was racked into casks in the basement. The brewery at Cote Hill had no less than seven storeys (Figure 5) and the rating valuations for 1865 and 1886 give some impression of the scale of the new buildings when compared with those they replaced.[22]

Figure 5. The Victoria Brewery around 1932. *Mark Heap Collection*

Warley Valuation 1865 (Old Brewery)

Owner	Occupier	Location	Description	Sq Yds	Gross Value		
					£	s	d
John Wigglesworth	John Naylor	Green Hills	Victoria Brewery				
			Cellar	137	11	19	9
			Ale Cellar	50	1	13	4
			Brewery & Malt Chambers	74	8	0	4
			Brewery & Malt Chambers	25	2	10	0
			Offices & Joiners Shop	24	2	14	0
			Porter vat	18	1	7	0
			Cart Shed	56	1	8	0
			Stable & Loft	51	3	16	6
			Coach House etc.		2	14	0
			Kitchen			6	0
					36	**8**	**0**

Warley Valuation 1886 (New Brewery)

Owner	Occupier	Description		Sq Yds	Gross Value		
					£	s	d
John Naylor	John Naylor	Covered Yard & Shed Albion Brewery		225	11	5	0
		Brewhouse	7 storeys	72	28	15	0
		Square Room & Hop Warehouse	3 storeys	154	27	0	0
		Offices	1 storey	40	3	0	0
		Stables, Cooperage	1 storey	174	10	0	0
		Hay & Corn Room Over	1 storey	154	7	15	0
		Store Room Over	1 storey	200	10	0	0
		Cellars above Brewery	1 storey	300	11	5	0
		Engine Power, Boiler etc.			20	0	0
		Stable			2	5	0
					131	**5**	**0**

It will be seen that in 1865 the owner of the land was Josiah Wigglesworth, but that in 1886 Naylor had secured the freehold to his brewery premises, and that once the building work was completed the name of the premises was changed to the Albion Brewery. The 'cellars above brewery' probably indicates cellars built into the hillside behind the main buildings. The valuation also reveals that one of the products was porter; an important part of the Sowerby

Figure 6. The former Maltings of the Victoria Brewery is visible behind the auto showroom, 1984. *P W Robinson*

Figure 7. Another view of the former Maltings, 1980. *P W Robinson*

Bridge trade at this time, it was brewed by both the Calderdale Brewery, Mearclough, and the Bank Brewery, Wharf Street, both in Sowerby Bridge. By the end of the nineteenth century this beer style had all but disappeared.

Further additions were made to the brewery premises in 1876, when a substantial floor maltings to the designs of T W Helliwell was erected on the hillside behind (Figures 6 & 7).[23]

Halifax Borough Valuation, Warley Ward 1901[24]

Owner	Occupier	Description	Sq Yds	Gross Value		
				£	s	d
John Naylor	John Naylor	Malt Kiln	2 storeys	14	10	0
		Top Floor Attic	½ storey	23	0	0
		Growing Room	1 storey	23	0	0
		Growing Room	1 sorey	23	0	0
				83	**10**	**0**

With his business flourishing, John Naylor was able to take an active role in local affairs, being the last surviving member of the old Board of Surveyors for Warley. He was associated with Sowerby Bridge Local Board from 1861-77, and its chairman in 1871. During his office he was involved in successful efforts to remove tolls from both the Rochdale and Tuel Lane turnpikes as well as obtaining powers for the widening of Burnley Road and also County Bridge at Sowerby Bridge.[25] In contrast to these good works as a pillar of the local community, Naylor's character was not flawless; as a younger man he had been fined £5 for the indecent assault of Mrs Ann Goodwin, wife of a railway porter from Sowerby Bridge, in a railway carriage at North Dean Station.[26]

As John Naylor's fortune increased he was able to live in some style at Fern Hill, Warley, with his wife and seven daughters. During 1886 he also acquired the lease of the mansion at Ash Grove, near Elland, with its extensive grounds, formerly occupied by Major Edwards, together with some adjoining farmland.[27] Throughout this period a manager looked after Naylor's business interests at the brewery and eventually the Halifax Brewery Company was formed to carry on the activities there. Thomas Greenwood of Gibbet Street was the company's brewer and manager by 1899 and he is named on the deed transferring the pubs and beer-houses to James Alderson & Co Ltd in 1910. It seems that the two companies may have already been closely associated by this time, for the deed of transfer gives the Alderson company's registered address as Warley Springs Brewery, under which name the Albion Brewery was by then known. Significantly the brewery premises were not included in the deal, so perhaps the Alderson company had previously transferred operations to Cote Hill and was already brewing for Halifax Brewery Company houses.

With its acquisition of the Halifax Brewery Company, the enlarged business now controlled some 53 pubs and beerhouses, giving it a tied estate comparable with some of the big names in Halifax brewing at that time, such as Richard Whitaker of Seedlings Mount Brewery and Brear & Brown of Hipperholme. Amongst the properties acquired was the Windmill beer-house, the Hough, which stood adjacent to the brewery premises at Northowram. Within a short time the operations at Windmill were closed down and all production transferred to the much larger premises at Cote Hill.[28]

Unfortunately the merger brought only short-term benefits in terms of profitability before further problems were to hit the brewing industry during the first world war. Duty on beer was increased by 300 per cent, licensing hours were introduced and raw material became difficult to obtain. These circumstances brought about the spectacular failure of Brear & Brown of Hipperholme in 1916 following a petition by creditors. Other competitors were faring little better, many ceasing to pay dividends to their shareholders. Although reductions in beer strength and rising prices enabled profits to recover towards the end of the war, it was not enough to prevent the acceptance of an offer by the Alderson board of an offer by Thomas Ramsden & Son Ltd for the whole of the company's assets in 1919.

Thus the business empire which had been established by James Alderson at Lower Brear finally came to an end. The brewery premises at Cote Hill were used for a number of years as a dye house, the tower eventually being demolished in June 1963.[29] Most of the site is now occupied by a petrol station, though the former malting premises still survive on the hillside behind.

Notes and References

1. *Halifax Guardian*, 7 November 1908.
2. *Halifax Courier*, 3 November 1866.
3. West Yorkshire Archive Service, Calderdale District Archive (WYAS Calderdale), BRA:490 Purchase agreement re Tan House Field and Brewery dated 17 September 1851.
4. *Halifax Guardian*, 8 April 1876.
5. WYAS Calderdale, CM/1881-1885.
6. P W Robinson, 'Emergence of Common Brewers in the Halifax District', *Transactions of the Halifax Antiquarian Society (THAS)*, 1981; K H Hawkins & C L Pass, *The Brewing Industry*, 1979.
7. P W Robinson, *A History of the Fountain Head Brewery*, 1988. Unpub. account produced for Samuel Webster & Wilsons Ltd. A copy is deposited with the Halifax Central Library Reference Department.
8. It was usual for breweries to charge their licensed tenants two types of rent. A 'dry' rent represented a rent based on the value of the premises, and a 'wet' rent which varied according to the barrelage of the pub or beer-house.
9. WYAS Wakefield District Archive Deed Registry (WYAS Wakefield), 1901 Vol 4, p 956, No 417.
10. P W Robinson, 'Joseph Frederick Walsh (1861-1950), Architect: His Early Career', *THAS*, Vol 9, 2001.
11. *Building News*, 19 November 1897.
12. WYAS Wakefield, 1901 Vol 4, p 956. No 417.
13. *Halifax Guardian*, 6 January 1906.
14. P W Robinson, *A History of the Fountain Head Brewery*, 1988.

15. *Halifax Courier*, 15 & 17 October 1974, suggest that bottling took place in Dewsbury. It would seem far more likely, however, that bottles were brought to Northowram for the work to be carried out there under the direct supervision of brewery employees.

16. *Halifax Guardian*, 7 November 1908.

17. P W Robinson, 'Emergence of Common Brewers in the Halifax District', *THAS*, 1981.

18. WYAS Wakefield, 1910 Vol 34, p 66, No 29.

19. *Halifax Guardian*, 1 May 1852.

20. *Halifax Courier*, 18 June 1864.

21. T Pike & Co, *Halifax and District Illustrated*, c.1900.

22. WYAS Calderdale, HXT:725, Warley valuation 1865 and HXT:726, Warley valuation 1886.

23. *Halifax Guardian*, 14 October 1876.

24. WYAS Calderdale, HXT:183/3, Halifax Borough Valuation, Warley ward 1901.

25. *Halifax Guardian*, 9 December 1912.

26. *Halifax Courier*, 17 April 1858.

27. *Halifax Courier*, 16 October 1886.

28. *Halifax Courier*, 20 October 1974. Mr F L Bradley recalls that his father (aged 83 in 1974) worked at Windmill Brewery as an office boy on leaving school. He did not work there long and the brewery did not exist very much longer after he finished.

29. *Halifax Courier*, 29 June 1963.

List of Public House & Beerhouses owned by James Alderson and James Alderson & Co. Ltd.

List of Houses Transferred to James Alderson & Co. Ltd. on the Formation of the Company 29 December 1900 (Deed registry 1900 Vol. 4, p. 956, no. 417)

Name	Address	Type of Licence	Date of Conveyance	Purchaser	Notes
Sportsman Inn	Near Beech Street & Granville Street, Clayton, Bradford	bh	11.05.1874	S & A	Closed
Hen & Chickens	20 Winding Road, Halifax	bh	13.03.1885	A	Closed 1911
Victoria & Albert Inn and eight cottages	Victoria Street & Albert Street, Haley Hill, Northowram	bh	19.08.1887	A	Closed 1931
Oddfellows Arms	Clayton Road & Beck Side Road, Lidget Green, Bradford	bh	01.04.1895	A	
Rose & Crown	35 Cote Hill, Halifax	bh	17.03.1897	A	Closed 1941
Who Could a Thowt It	Sunny Bank Lane, Southowram	bh	27.05.1898	A	Closed 1933
Bridge Tavern	Briggate, Brighouse	bh	01.06.1900	A	Closed 1974

List of Properties sold by Halifax Brewery Co. to James Alderson & Co. Ltd. on 6 July 1910 (Deed Registry 1910 Vol. 34, p. 66, no. 29)

Name	Address	Type of Licence	Date of Conveyance/ Orig. Lease	Purchaser	Tenure	Notes
Barley Mow (former), shops & cottage	Westgate, Elland	bh	01.04.1854	JB	L	Closed 1898
Woodman Inn & eight cottages	Brookfoot	bh	09.05.1854		L	Closed 1941
Prospect Tavern	Wakefield Road, Bradford		23.02.1860	JN	F	Closed
Navigation	47 Chapel Lane, Sowerby Bridge	bh	08.06.1861	JN	F	
Mechanics Arms (former)	Winding Road, Halifax	bh	19.08.1865	JN	F	Closed 1905
Junction Inn	Toothill Bank, Rastrick	full	24.08.1867	JN	F	$
			24.09.1867	JN	F	
			09.02.1892	JN	F	
Miners Arms (former)	2 Bridge Street East, Cripplegate, Halifax	bh	01.07.1871	JN	F	Closed 1903
Black Bull	Heptonstall	full	09.11.1971	JN	F	Closed 1919

Name	Location	Type	Date		Code	Status
New Rock	Brick Green, Scammonden Road, Barkisland	bh	02.12.1871	JN	F	
Black Boy Inn (former)	King Cross Lane, Halifax	bh	01.02.1873	JN	F	Closed 1908
Moorcock Inn	Shaws Lane	full	24.06.1873	JN	F	Closed 1914
			01.10.1873	JN	F	
			03.11.1877	JN	F	
Spread Eagle	Butts Green, Rishworth	full	03.01.1874	JN	F	Closed 1948
Talbot Inn	Rawfolds, Liversedge, Birstal		25.02.1874	JN	F	Closed
Beehive Inn	Buttershaw	bh	10.10.1874	JN	F	
Stotts Arms	Brighouse	full	21.10.1874	JN	F	Closed 1998
Albion Inn	Scarr Head Road, Norland	full	12.02.1876	JN	F	Closed 1950
Rock Tavern	Upper Edge, Elland	full	15.09.1876	JN	F	
Forresters Arms	Kitson Lane, Norland	bh	12.10.1878	JN	F	Closed 1939
Two houses (formerly Victoria Arms)	15 & 17 King Street, Halifax	bh	13.12.1878	JN	L	Closed 1905
Pineberry Tavern	Halifax	bh	20.01.1879	JN	F	Closed 1925
Grocer's shop	17 Willow Hall Lane, Skircoat	off	01.12.1879	JN	F	
Prince of Wales	Salterhebble, Halifax	bh	pre 1881		L	Closed 1962
Blue Ball Inn	Jemmy Lane, North Bridge, Halifax	full	24.05.1884	JN	F	Closed 1915
Blue Ball Inn	Norland	full	24.05.1884	JN	F	
Windmill Inn	1 Park Square, Hough, Northowram	bh	24.05.1884	JN	F	
White Horse Inn	Bowling Back Lane, Bradford	full	21.06.1884	JN	F	
Waterhouse Arms & property formerly Victoria Inn	King Street, Halifax	full	13.10.1884	JN	L	Closed 1929
White Lion Inn (former)	Bridge End, Rastrick	full	18.02.1885	JN	L	Closed 1908
Grocer's Shop	19 Church Street, Halifax	off	04.09.1888	JN	F	
New Inn (former)	Holdsworth Street, Lower Shaw Hill, Halifax	bh	20.12.1888	JN	F	Closed 1908
Beehive Inn	Royd Lane, Soyland	full	27.07/1889	JN	F	
Golden Plough (former) & shop	Elland Lane/Quebec Street, Elland	full	13.12.1890	JN	F	Closed 1907
Waiters Arms	Tuel Lane, Sowerby Bridge	bh	14.07.1891	JN	F	
New Inn	Albert Street/Nelson Street/Union Street, Low Moor	full	02.09.1891	JN	F	
Swan Bank Tavern	Swan Bank Lane, Halifax	bh	01.05.1895	JN	F	Closed 1977
Duke of Wellington (former)	14 King Street, Halifax	bh	10.03.1896	JN	F	Closed 1905
Royal George	Towngate, Midgley	bh	17.04.1896	JN	F	Closed 1919
New Inn & shops	Briggate, Elland	full	26.07.1897	JD	F	Closed 1957
Hole in the Wall	Hangingroyd Lane, Hebden Bridge	full	22.02.1897	TG	F	$
Elephant & Castle	Hawksclough, Mytholmroyd	full	23.12.1897	TG	F	Closed
Land & stable	Hawksclough, Mytholmroyd	-	23.12.1897		L	
White Lion	Water Hill, Warley	bh	19.11.1898	JD	F	Closed 1948
House & shop	63 King Cross Street, Halifax	off	04.05.1899	JD	F	

List of Properties owned by John Naylor which eventually passed to Thomas Ramsden & Son Ltd. but which did not form part of the sale to James Alderson & Co. Ltd. in 1910

Name	Address	Type of Licence	Notes
Bridge Street Hotel	Bridge Street, Sowerby Bridge	bh	Closed 1951
Reed inn	46 West Street, Sowerby Bridge	bh	Closed 1928
Bulls Head Inn	Town Hall Street, Sowerby Bridge	full	
Engineers	72 Wharf Street, Sowerby Bridge	bh	
Branch Inn	15 Wharf Street, Sowerby Bridge	bh	Closed 1949
Delvers	Collier Topping, Boothtown, Halifax	bh	Closed 1925
Waggoners Rest	Stocks Lane, Warley	bh	Closed 1958
Delvers Arms	Brookfoot Lane, Southowram	full	Closed 1946
King Arms	Boulderclough, Sowerby	full	Closed 1989

Further Public Houses and Beerhouses known to have been operated by John Naylor

Name	Address	Type of Licence	Notes
Strangers Home	Clark Bridge, Halifax	bh	Demol.1899
Dublin Arms (aka Waggon & Horses)	Berry Lane, Halifax	bh	Closed 1905
Football	Elland Road, Brighouse	bh	Closed 1926
Abbey Inn	Abbey Lane, Newlands, Luddenden	bh	Closed 1911
Forresters Arms	Brook Street, Luddenden	bh	Closed 1903
Cherry Tree	Wall Nook, Barkisland	bh	Closed
Waggon & Horses	74 West Street, Sowerby Bridge	bh	Closed 1907
Rose & Crown	Oldham Road, Ripponden	bh	Closed 1911

Notes

Types of Licence	bh = beerhouse; off = off licence; full = fully licenced	
Purchaser	S & A = Shepherd & Alderson	
	A = James Alderson	
	JB = Joseph Brear	
	JN = John Naylor	
	JD = James Duff, shareholder of Halifax Brewery Co.	
	TG = Thomas Greenwood & Joseph Henry Finlinson, shareholders of Halifax Brewery Co.	
Tenure	L = leasehold, F = freehold	
$	The Hole in the Wall, Hebden Bridge was rebuilt by the Halifax Brewery Co. in 1898 and the Junction, Rastrick in 1899.	

6. WHEN THE CHIEFS CAME TO TOWN: THREE AFRICAN CHIEFS VISIT HALIFAX – OCTOBER 1895

by Jill Robinson

THE PRESENT-DAY COUNTRY OF BOTSWANA in Southern Africa, formerly the British Protectorate of Bechuanaland, is proud of the fact that it was never colonised, but that its tribal lands were permitted to remain under their traditional form of government. That this is the case is due in part to the visit made to England over a hundred years ago by three Bechuana chiefs, who held meetings with sympathisers in various towns and cities, including Halifax.

The chiefs - Khama of the BaMangwato (erroneously referred to in contemporary accounts as 'King Khama'), Sebele and Bathoen, were assisted by the London Missionary Society, which had been active in Bechuanaland converting a number of the tribal people to Christianity. The missionaries, in common with the Temperance Movement, supported the chiefs in their desire to thwart the plans of Cecil Rhodes, who wished to annexe their tribal lands and administer them through his South Africa Company, in order to further his plans for a railway running from the Cape of Good Hope to Cairo in Egypt. This 'Cape to Cairo' project would open up the interior of the continent of Africa for mineral exploitation and further colonisation. However, the chiefs argued that if they allowed Rhodes to have his way, his employees would bring alcoholic drink into Bechuanaland, which was something they wished to avoid. They permitted their own native beers to be drunk, but did not want European spirits in their lands; these views therefore ensured the support of the Temperance Movement.

The story of the visit of the three chiefs has been documented by Neil Parsons of the University of Botswana, in his book *King Khama, Emperor Joe and the Great White Queen*.[1] He made use of a file of press clippings kept by Bathoen throughout most of the journey. However, although mention is made of the fact that the three visited Halifax, no details are given. This led me to wonder what exactly had occurred in Halifax and whether anything had been reported in the local paper.

Accordingly, I visited the Halifax Central Reference Library, where copies of the *Halifax Courier* are kept on microfilm. Two

Figure 1. Khama in western clothes during his visit (after Edwin Lloyd, *Three Great African Chiefs*).

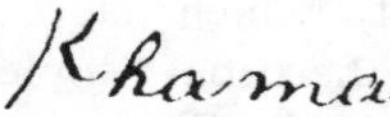

Khama

Figure 2. 'King' Khama's signature.

reports were found therein, one concerning the meeting held in the Mechanics' Hall (now the YMCA buildings) on 29 October 1895, and the other of an interview given by Sebele and Bathoen the previous day.[2] Khama (Figures 1 & 2) was not available for the interview, being away fox-hunting in Nottinghamshire at the time the *Courier* correspondent called to interview the Africans! The interview took place at Greenroyds, the home of the Whitley family, where they were staying during their Halifax sojourn.

I took copies of these reports from the microfilm and forwarded them to Professor Parsons in Gaborone, capital of Botswana. He confessed that this material was indeed new to him, as he only had access to the incomplete file of press cuttings kept by Bathoen and brought back to Bechuanaland. Professor Parsons had not yet had an opportunity to visit England to check local papers as possible sources of information about the visit.

The *Courier* accounts proved very interesting. It was in Halifax that these men first encountered snow; a snowball was actually produced from the lawn of Greenroyd and brought indoors for them to examine, which they are reported to have done 'with great curiosity'. The interview had to be conducted through an interpreter, the Reverend W C Willoughby, as none of the chiefs spoke English. When asked about their worst and best experiences in Britain, they all agreed that the worst aspect was the cold weather (their lands, after all, lay for the most part in the tropics), whereas their best experience was said to be 'the people, who receive a stranger most kindly, and are pleased to do everything they can for him'.

It is worth noting that in those days at the end of the nineteenth century, before political correctness, the newspaper could note the 'dusky complexions and woolly hair' of the African visitors, who were splendidly attired in typical Victorian gentlemen's garb of frock coats and top hats, purchased upon their arrival in London. The reporter went on to enquire as to which women, English or African, they thought most beautiful. It is unlikely, I feel, that such a question would be asked today - nor indeed should it be! However, Bathoen is reported to have replied, perhaps in true diplomatic manner, that an Englishwoman is to be preferred, as she has 'fine clothes, a fine nose, a pretty mouth and handsome teeth, and she washes every morning'. Professor Parsons commented, on learning of this remark, that the chief would have been impressed by women 'all dolled up'.

He also noted that in one important respect the remark about washing reflected an aspect of Britain which would have astounded the Africans, whose life experience was of an arid territory on the edge of the Kalahari desert - the abundance of water was a shock to them. The chiefs went on to tell the reporter that they were looking forward to meeting Queen Victoria, declaring 'we shall rejoice when we see her'.

The account of the meeting at the Mechanics' Hall in Halifax opens with the following paragraph, not written in the snappy prose style now expected of the popular press, but more typical of its day:

Probably the predominant motive which actuated a large number of people who crowded the Mechanics' Hall last evening was one of sheer curiosity to see and hear the Bechuana King, Khama, and the chiefs Bathoen and Sebele, whose errand to this country appeals strongly to an Englishman's sense of right and justice: and judging by the enthusiasm shown there could scarcely be anyone who, at any rate as the mission of the swarthy visitors was made clear, was not in thorough sympathy with them in their efforts to retain the management of their own affairs on their native soil. The keenest interest was manifested in the event, and by six o'clock numbers were clamouring for admission; while long before 730, the time announced for the meeting to start, the accommodation of the hall was taxed to the utmost. Hundreds of people, unable to gain admission, lined the corridors and staircases, and it was with no small amount of difficulty that a late comer could worm his way along the congested passages.

Inside the hall, the scene was inspiring to a degree - platform area and gallery being chockfull of expectant faces... Naturally, the African potentates were the great attraction, and from the moment of their appearance they were subjected to the scrutinising gaze of the vast audience... they were greeted with hearty cheers and a high pitch of enthusiasm was maintained all through the meeting.[2]

Reverend Willoughby gave what was recorded as a 'good-humoured, sensible speech', after which each of the three chiefs spoke in turn, via the interpreter. Bathoen opened with 'I rejoice to stand before this assembly' and went on to explain the purpose of the visit and the nature of the struggle against Rhodes' Standard Chartered

Company, after which he received an ovation. He was followed by Sebele, who recounted how earlier in the century he had met the celebrated missionaries David Livingstone and Robert Moffat; he also emphasised the chiefs' opposition to drink. He too received warm applause. Finally it was Khama's turn to speak; as he rose to address the meeting the audience also rose *en masse*, and cheered him with great enthusiasm. Khama explained that he was tired after his exertions in the hunting field earlier that day and apparently went on to say 'we are all people, and we were moulded by God, and He gave us the land wherein we live that it might be our land and we should live in it'. He also was given a magnificent reception.

After all the speeches had finished, a resolution was passed unanimously endorsing the chiefs' petition and many people signed a memo to Joseph Chamberlain, the Colonial Secretary (Figure 3).

In those days, prior to the advent of mass communication and also predating the era when foreign travel became widely accessible, the impact of a visit by three such exotic personages to a small provincial

Figure 3. Khama (left) and Sebele (right) with the Lord Provost Glasgow (centre), 24 October 1895
Glasgow Times, *25 October 1895*

town must have been remarkable indeed. The chiefs went on to meet Queen Victoria and Joseph Chamberlain, and their mission was judged a success; although it was probably the disastrous raid into Boer-held territory led by Rhodes' friend, Dr Leander Starr Jameson, which finally demolished Rhodes' plan to bring Bechuanaland under the control of his Chartered Company.

In all events the chiefs' land was never colonised, but became a protectorate, the most minimal association with the British Empire, which allowed traditional structures to be maintained. Thus, when Bechuanaland became the independent country of Botswana in 1966, this was achieved for the most part without the civil unrest which blighted the independence struggles of many fully colonised African countries; and, more than thirty-five years later, it continues to be a peaceful place.

Notes and References

1. Parsons, Neil. *King Khama, Emperor Joe and the Great White Queen.* University of Chicago Press, 1998.
2. *Halifax Courier*, 29 October 1895; 30 October 1895.
Acknowledgment: with thanks to staff at Halifax Central Reference Library.

7. GUNS AND ROSES: BENJAMIN WILSON (1824–97) OF SALTERHEBBLE, CHARTIST AND HORTICULTURIST

by John A Hargreaves

IN MAY 1848, the year of revolutions across Europe, Benjamin Wilson, the Salterhebble Chartist, bought himself a gun.[1] As he explained nearly forty years later in his autobiography: 'a great many people in these districts were arming themselves with guns or pikes, and drilling on the moors' during a year which saw revolution engulf virtually the whole of Europe outside Britain and Russia. A close friend of Wilson's was busy moulding bullets in his cellar and Wilson was persuaded by Bill Cockroft, 'one of the leaders of the physical force party in Halifax', to identify with that section of the movement, now becoming dominant in Halifax Chartism, which saw resort to arms as a legitimate means of achieving the Chartist political programme of the vote for all adult males plus five other demands for reform of the electoral system listed in the famous *People's Charter* of 1838. However, Wilson's decision to purchase a gun for such a purpose was not taken lightly. Indeed, he professed some reservations, realising that it was 'a serious thing for a Chartist to have a gun or a pike in his possession', but frustration with the peremptory rejection of the third Chartist national petition containing 5,706,000 signatures on 10 April 1848 appeared to suggest no other alternative in the heady atmosphere of that tumultuous year.[2]

It was not that Wilson lacked experience in the use of firearms. 'I had several years' practice in shooting', he explained in his memoirs, 'as the farmer for whom I worked supplied me with gun, powder, and shot for the purpose of shooting birds in summer' and he eagerly awaited instructions from Cockroft 'how to proceed until wanted'. In the event, however, Wilson's apparent readiness to put his commitment to physical-force Chartism to the test in May was never required as 'the scheme was abandoned'.[3] Moreover, next month, Wilson and two Halifax friends remained unarmed when forced to flee over a wall pursued by mounted troops 'with drawn swords slashing in all directions' in the turmoil following a huge Chartist open-air meeting at Toftshaw Moor, four miles to the south of

Bradford on 12 June 1848, where 'physical force was strongly advocated' and 'the people were recommended to arm themselves'.[4] 'It might now be said', Wilson later wrote in 1887, that 'we were fools, but ... young people now have no idea of what we had to endure'.[5] He was then writing, however, from the perspective of a well-respected Gladstonian Liberal, temperance advocate and enthusiastic propagandist of the inoffensive art of rose cultivation, some two years after the enactment of the *Third Reform Act*, which had established a uniform household and lodger franchise in counties and boroughs throughout the United Kingdom, increasing the franchise by 72 per cent from 3.3 million to 5.7 million, abolished the property qualification for MPs and made the first systematic attempt to relate parliamentary representation to population size in an ensuing *Redistribution Act*, thereby responding in some degree to several key points in the Chartist programme.[6]

What were the circumstances in Wilson's early life and experience which first drew him into the Chartist Movement and why did he later espouse mid-Victorian Liberalism, teetotalism, and horticulture.

Wilson was born on 7 August 1824 of humble parentage at Skircoat Green, a village on the southern perimeter of Halifax, which Wilson acknowledged 'had long been noted for its Radicalism'. His autobiography, (Figure 1) which makes no reference to his father, reveals that, six years before her son's birth, his mother had gone into mourning 'for the victims of Peterloo'. Here, at a radical reform meeting at St Peter's Fields, Manchester, on 16 August 1819, eleven protesters had been killed and over 400 others, including women and children, had suffered injuries after the yeomanry had attempted to break up the demonstration and arrest the speaker, Orator Henry Hunt.

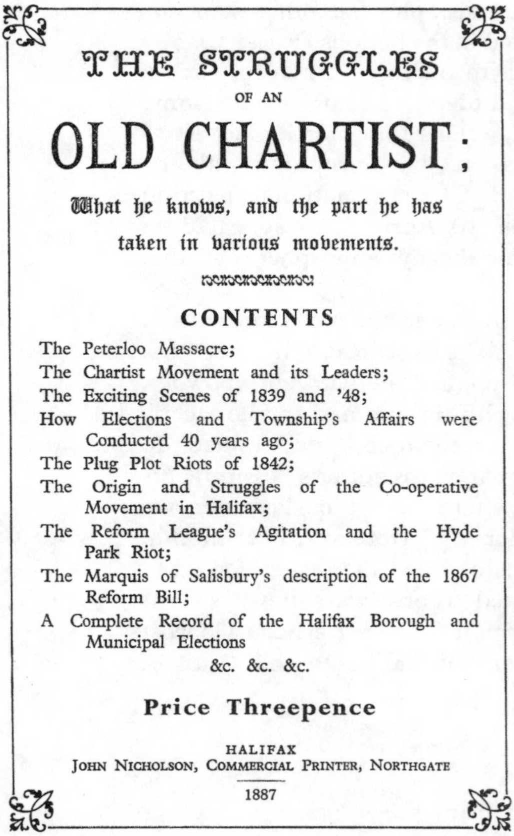

THE STRUGGLES
OF AN
OLD CHARTIST:

What he knows, and the part he has taken in various movements.

CONTENTS

The Peterloo Massacre;
The Chartist Movement and its Leaders;
The Exciting Scenes of 1839 and '48;
How Elections and Township's Affairs were Conducted 40 years ago;
The Plug Plot Riots of 1842;
The Origin and Struggles of the Co-operative Movement in Halifax;
The Reform League's Agitation and the Hyde Park Riot;
The Marquis of Salisbury's description of the 1867 Reform Bill;
A Complete Record of the Halifax Borough and Municipal Elections
&c. &c. &c.

Price Threepence

HALIFAX
JOHN NICHOLSON, COMMERCIAL PRINTER, NORTHGATE
1887

Figure 1. Title page of Benjamin Wilson's *The Struggles of an Old Chartist*, published in Halifax in 1887. *J A Hargreaves Collection*

The shock waves from Peterloo were felt on both sides of the Pennines and Wilson's mother was one of many women who were drawn into radical politics in the aftermath of the massacre. She attended a protest meeting at the home of Thomas Washington, a radical shoemaker, in Skircoat Green and later joined a procession, marching 'in solemn silence' behind Washington's wife, who held aloft 'a cap of liberty on the top of a pole' as hundreds paraded through the streets of Halifax to a meeting near Huddersfield. One of Benjamin Wilson's uncles, like other villagers, 'wore grey hats with weeds around them' as symbols of mourning. Wilson surmised that his mother's radical instincts, awakened by her sense of outrage at the conduct of the authorities at Peterloo, sprang partly from the poverty of her own upbringing, when she had been obliged to eke out a living pounding sand for a neighbour and subsisting upon a diet of boiled potato peelings. A continuing radical tradition in Skircoat Green, reinforced by the experience of Peterloo, provided Wilson with some of his own earliest memories when he recalled 'the great rejoicing' which followed the passing of the first *Reform Bill* in 1832, when the Skircoat Green band was engaged by the Liberals, who proclaimed themselves the friends of the poor people. 'The only reason that I had for being yellow was that I was poor' recalled Wilson 'and they were my friends'.[7]

Wilson never attended day school in his life, but learned to read at the Wesleyan Sunday School at Skircoat Green, which besides being a stronghold of radicalism was also an early centre of Methodism.[8] Indeed, Methodist preaching had taken place in the out-township of Skircoat some seven years before John Wesley first preached in the market place at Halifax in 1748. John Nelson, the Birstall stonemason who became one of the most celebrated of Wesley's army of lay preachers, had delivered the first Methodist sermon on an upturned washtub beneath the Rocks at Skircoat in 1741, with the river Calder murmuring in the valley below. And later in 1748 when a mob stirred up by a member of the local gentry disrupted Wesley's preaching in Halifax, his journal records that he retired mud-bespattered and bleeding to a field near Salterhebble, where he resumed his sermon.[9] Although Wilson was critical of some aspects of Sunday School education, for example the reluctance of some schools to teach writing on the Sabbath and the ready resort to corporal punishment by some teachers, he acknowledged that he owed all his early learning to the Sunday School which provided many of his generation with 'the only chance we had' to acquire the rudiments of an education. As a young man the culture of the chapel would have broadened this rudimentary education, and in 1839 he recalled having heard William Thornton, a radical Methodist lay preacher, lecture at the Wesleyan School at Skircoat Green. Indeed, it is possible that his growing interest in radicalism during the 1830s may have been nurtured by a generation of Methodist preachers who also embraced radical politics, like Thornton, who lived for a time in Skircoat Green.[10]

Wilson was put to work at an early age as a farm labourer, rising before dawn to milk cows, and also engaged in the extensive domestic outwork system of card-setting, for which he received a mere halfpenny for setting some 1,500 teeth in hand cards used in the preparation of wool for spinning. His own continuing experience of hardship strengthened his growing radical sympathies. He later wound bobbins for his uncle, Joseph Wilson, a small piece maker of Skircoat Green, whose wife, 'a famous politician, a Chartist and a great admirer of Fergus O'Connor' first aroused his interest in the Chartist movement, encouraging him to attend a large rally addressed by O'Connor at Hartshead Moor on Whit Monday 1839. Accompanied by a neighbour, Samuel Jackson, and 'a band of music', he marched in a huge procession via Godley Lane and Hipperholme, later providing in his autobiography a graphic description of the arrival of the Bradford contingent, led by Peter Bussey, 'on horseback, and wearing a green sash' as they climbed the hill above Bailiffe Bridge. At the meeting, the largest he ever attended, he recalled O'Connor's celebrated anti-clerical aside to William Thornton. After Thornton had opened the proceedings with prayer, O'Connor turned to him, clapping the Skircoat Green lay preacher on the shoulder and declaring: 'Well done, Thornton, when we get the People's Charter I will see that you are made the Archbishop of York'.[11]

Wilson regarded 1839, when no fewer than 13,036 signatures from the parish of Halifax were appended to the first Chartist national petition, as the peak of popular support for Chartism and also provided evidence of arming in the West Riding prior to the unsuccessful Newport Rising in Monmouthshire of November 1839, suggesting that a sympathetic rising might have been triggered in the West Riding had not the appointed leader Peter Bussey of Bradford fallen sick and disappeared from the scene 'into the country out of the way' or 'hiding in his warehouse among the sacks'. However, support for the National Charter Association grew rapidly in Halifax in 1841, attracting 460 members, and the extent and intensity of violence in Halifax in the summer of 1842 was greater than at any

Figure 2. Plug Rioters at North Bridge, Halifax, 15 August 1842. *Illustrated London News*

other point during the Chartist decade.

Indeed, Wilson provided an eye-witness account of the Plug Plot disturbances in Halifax in mid-August 1842 (Figure 2), which was followed by a violent attack on the military at Salterhebble (Figure 3), when three cavalrymen were hurled from their horses and kicked

Figure 3. Attack on the military at Salterhebble, Halifax, 16 August 1842. *Illustrated London News*

and beaten by an angry mob and order was restored only after troops opened fire on the crowd. 'At no time during the Chartist period', concluded the historian of public order during the Chartist era, F C Mather, 'had regular troops come nearer to being overwhelmed by rioters'. Wilson's account is significant in that he attributed the Salterhebble disturbances to 'young men from the districts surrounding' rather than plug rioters from Bradford or Lancashire.[12]

Wilson's autobiography affirmed the continuity of Chartism throughout the middle years of the decade, despite the subsequent dwindling membership of the National Charter Association. He records sitting on the committee 'for several years', recalling that 'we had no wealthy men amongst us' and 'no paid officials' and that 'even when the agitation was at its height very few of those attending its meetings joined the Association or subscribed to its funds'. He attributed the level of political interest to the popular impact of the *Northern Star*, which, he reveals, was read aloud in cottages to groups of domestic outworkers, such as handloom weavers and woolcombers, who formed the backbone of the local Chartist movement.

In 1848, when Halifax was rife with rumours of drilling following the outbreak of revolution in France in February, the most violent incidents occurred in Bradford, which F C Mather pronounced 'perhaps the most outstanding centre of physical force Chartism in England in the spring of 1848'. However, Wilson attributed the resurgence of Chartism in the 'year of agitations and revolutions', when 'thousands fell on the field of battle fighting for the people's cause in Europe in this struggle', as much to the recurrence of trade depression and soaring bread prices, echoing William Cobbett in his suggestion that 'the easiest way to get to an Englishman's brains is through his stomach'. He described a crowded meeting at the Odd Fellows Hall to commemorate the outbreak of the French Revolution where 'the resolutions put to the meeting were carried with great enthusiasm' and the large open-air meetings at Blackstone Edge, Skircoat Moor and Toftshaw Moor.[13]

During the 1840s Wilson earned an average weekly wage of nine shillings from a succession of jobs as a weaver, woolcomber, railway navvy and quarryman and was 'frequently short of the commonest of food'. He joined the Rose of the Valley lodge of a friendly society, the Independent Order of Oddfellows (Figure 4), and attempted to intervene in local township politics. When Wilson attended his first vestry meeting in the Skircoat township in 1843, he records that he was 'the only working man present' and that he 'felt uncomfortable'

Figure 4. Oddfellows Hall, Halifax. *J A Hargreaves Collection*

and wished he was 'nicely out'. He condemned the gentlemen who constituted the Board of Surveyors for always taking care that 'the roads near their own residences were kept in good repair, although the roads in other parts were in a wretched condition' and over the next ten to twelve years he campaigned for better representation of working class interests in township and later municipal politics, skilfully utilising statutes and byelaws to attack local vested interests. In the Halifax parliamentary elections of 1847 and 1852 Wilson supported the Chartist candidate Ernest Jones, with whom he developed a close personal friendship, which lasted for the remainder of Jones's life, representing the Halifax Branch of the Reform League at his funeral in Manchester in 1869.[14]

During the period between the demise of Chartism and the foundation of the Reform League, Wilson became increasingly involved in the co-operative movement and in 1849 'resolved not to taste of any intoxicating drink or smoke tobacco' as an example to others, in the belief that 'if working men could have been induced to invest in the co-operative movement what they were spending on intoxicating drinks it would have greatly improved their condition'.

He had met with Joseph Foreman and J D Taylor in 1848-49 in an abortive attempt to establish a Halifax Co-operative Trading Society. These enthusiastic co-operative pioneers bought two or three hundredweight of soap and sugar and made it up into one and two pound bags for sale within the society. However, the decision 'to pay no bonus but to add it to stock, so that it would become more powerful and give us more capital', proved unattractive to consumers and the scheme 'was not patronised as it ought to have been, so we had to abandon it and lose nearly all we had put in'. The scheme operated for only five months, when Wilson parted company with Taylor, who went on to become the founding secretary of the Halifax Permanent Benefit Building Society in February 1853.[15]

Wilson also identified with the campaign for secular education and later joined the Halifax Liberal Electoral Association, formed by supporters of Edward Owen Greening, the radical candidate at the 1868 Halifax Election, to look after the registration and organisation of radical interests in the borough. Wilson was one of two delegates from the lower division of Skircoat on its executive, which consisted of two delegates from each ward. After the election, in which Greening trailed the poll with 2,802 votes to James Stansfeld's 5,278 and Edward Akroyd's 5,141, Wilson supported the dissolution of the Halifax Liberal Electoral Association and the incorporation of all shades of Liberal opinion into the newly established Halifax Liberal Association. Wilson became a great admirer of William Gladstone and regarded his first ministry as 'the most Radical that we ever had in this country'. The Liberal government soon set to work, he recalled with approval, disestablishing the Irish Church, introducing the secret ballot, another of the Chartist six points, and carrying the *Education Act*.

In Halifax, Wilson campaigned energetically for a new Board School at Siddal, in the face of opposition from local Anglican-Tory elites. He subsequently played an increasingly prominent role in local Liberal politics, opposing the selection of Colonel Edward Akroyd as Liberal candidate for the 1874 election and forming part of a deputation which invited the carpet manufacturer, John Crossley, to contest the election for the Liberals. Crossley proved a popular choice, topping the poll with 5,563 votes. Wilson was also chairman of a committee, which organised a Halifax Liberal Club visit to Gladstone's home at Hawarden Castle in June 1879. Six years later, he also organised a reunion of twenty-two former Chartists, aged between sixty-two and seventy-six, at Maude's Temperance Hotel, Halifax, to commemorate the passing of the *Third Reform Act*. Like Robert Lowery, the Newcastle Chartist, Wilson had formed part of that strand of Chartism which fed into popular Liberalism and he spent his declining years denouncing the formation of the Independent Labour Party, which he feared would sap the strength of Liberalism.[16]

However, Wilson's energies in later life were increasingly consumed by his passion for horticulture and he became well-known as an adjudicator at local horticultural shows and for his expertise in the cultivation of dwarf hybrid perpetual roses, his favourite flowers. Skircoat Green, which had earlier gained a reputation for its radicalism and nonconformity, was enjoying a growing reputation by the mid-nineteenth century as a centre of horticulture under the patronage of successful industrialists such as Edward and Louis John Crossley, who had acquired mansions with large estates on the southern perimeter of the town. *White's Directory* of 1853 listed ten gardeners in Skircoat township, no fewer than six of whom were based in Salterhebble or Skircoat Green, and Wilson himself often supplemented his meagre income working as a gardener.

Wilson later recalled, in a series of articles on horticulture in the *Halifax Courier*, the earliest local flower shows at the *Old King Cross Inn* and the more recently opened *Copley Arms*, where working-class, amateur florists competed for the prize of a copper kettle for their displays of auriculas. These early shows, which attracted relatively few visitors, paved the way for the more spectacular shows of the Skircoat Floral and Horticultural Society and the Salterhebble and District Rose Association, of which Wilson was a founder member, contributing ten shillings and sixpence, with William Kippax and Henry Conway, to cover the cost of the launch of the new association at the *Falcon Inn*, Salterhebble, in 1879. The association's shows, held in the grounds of Farfield and later Spring Hall, attracted entries from throughout the North and Midlands by 1892, when Perkins and Sons of Coventry won the gold medal for the premier rose with a bloom of Charles Lefevre.[17]

Wilson dated the growing local demand for rose trees from around 1869, when 'working men' now began 'to grow rose trees in their gardens and have little greenhouses' and observed in the early 1890s that 'the demand for roses is a rapidly increasing one and is now an important trade'. He believed that his success as a cultivator of roses derived from planting them in November, sheltered from northerly and easterly winds in well-spaced, deep trenches, with a plentiful supply of well-rotted manure, which he was careful to ensure did not come into direct contact with the roots, and moderate pruning, unless the growth was exceptionally weak.

Wilson was one of the few Chartist autobiographers not to appear dismissive of the Chartist Land Plan, which had sought to settle working men on the land as small freeholders during the period from 1845 to 1851, believing that 'the scheme was before its time' and that 'the day is not far distant when it will be successfully carried out'. He took a keen interest in the Halifax co-operative farm at High Sunderland in the mid-1860s when he served as a director of the Halifax Industrial Society, regularly visiting the farm and the newly constructed slaughter-house, which provided 'good tillage for the farm'.[18]

Gregarious by nature and a gifted and witty raconteur and writer, Wilson was known affectionately as Old Ben. Surprisingly, no likeness or even physical description of him has survived, though a journalist provided a rare glimpse of his domestic circumstances in his declining years. When he visited the veteran politician at his home in Chapel Street, Salterhebble, Wilson was sitting in his armchair by his hearth beneath a portrait of Ernest Jones the Chartist (Figure 5), flanked by portraits of his other heroes, William Gladstone and John Bright.[19]

Wilson died in dramatic circumstances at a tea party for the elderly in honour of Queen Victoria's Diamond Jubilee at Salterhebble United Methodist Free Church (Figure 6) on 21 June 1897, shortly before the arrival of the Mayor and Mayoress of Halifax at the conclusion of their official round of visits to the various municipal celebrations. After reminiscing, amidst much hilarity, about an inebriated woman's conduct in seeking to replenish her 'rum punch' at local celebrations to mark Queen Victoria's accession in 1837, Wilson suddenly collapsed and died from heart failure, having declared that he felt 'a funny sensation' and would 'have to

Figure 5. Ernest Jones (1819-69).
J A Hargreaves Collection

sit down'. The veteran radical, whose death occurred on a public platform on a national holiday to celebrate the longest reign in British history, was mourned as 'a Cromwell in the cause of progress and liberty'. His funeral and burial at All Saints Church, Salterhebble, was attended by a veteran Chartist, serving Liberal aldermen and councillors and members of the Salterhebble and District Rose Association, each of whom wore white roses in their button holes as a mark of respect.[20] A memorial service was later held at the Salterhebble United Methodist Free Church, where tribute was paid to his 'honest and straightforward' desire 'to do good in his day and generation'.

His widow, Mary Jane (1825-1907), whom he had married in 1854, had been almost blind from childhood and her straitened circumstances prompted an appeal which raised over £30 for a tombstone which bore the inscription: 'erected by public subscription to the memory of one who strove for the civil and social welfare of his fellow men'.[21]

Few nineteenth century radicals who, like Wilson, never attended a day school in his life gained such a reputation as he did as both a writer and public speaker. He remains the archetypal, self-taught working-man who articulated the hopes and fears of a generation experiencing the turbulent transition from a semi-rural, hierarchically structured community into an urban-industrial fledgling democracy. In 1848 he had been excited by the abdication of

Figure 6. Salterhebble United Methodist Free Church. *J A Hargreaves Collection*

King Louis-Philippe and the proclamation of a republic in Paris and persuaded briefly that it might be necessary to resort to arms in order to achieve democratic rights for the masses in England. By 1897 many of the aspirations he had cherished half a century earlier had been fulfilled by reforming Liberal governments after 1867 and he had diverted his energies into the cultivation of roses, which he regarded as 'the Queen of flowers'. He died celebrating the sixtieth anniversary of the accession to the throne of the Queen who had been removed to the Isle of Wight for her own safety in the anxious days of April 1848, when thousands of Chartists had descended on the capital in a final abortive attempt to secure the adoption of their third national petition, and was carried to his grave by crowds wearing symbolic roses in their buttonholes rather than parading caps of liberty.

Notes and References

1. This article is based upon research undertaken for the *New Dictionary of National Biography*, scheduled for publication in 2004, which will include, for the first time, an entry on Benjamin Wilson. A copy of the original 1887 edition of Benjamin Wilson's autobiography, *The Struggles of an Old Chartist*, is held in the Horsfall Turner Collection, Calderdale Central Library, and is reprinted in full in D Vincent, ed., *Testaments of Radicalism: Memoirs of Working Class Politicians, 1790-1885*, Europa, 1977. General introductions to Chartism and the social and economic context of the movement within Halifax are provided in Dorothy Thompson, *The Chartists* (Maurice Temple Smith, 1984) and J A Hargreaves, *Halifax* (Edinburgh University Press/Carnegie Publishing, 1999).
2. Vincent, *Testaments*, p 209.
3. *Ibid.*
4. *Ibid*, p 207; D G Wright, *The Chartist Risings in Bradford*, (Bradford Libraries, 1987), pp 54-55.
5. Vincent, Testaments, p 209.
6. E J Evans, *Parliamentary Reform, c1770-1918*, (Longman, 2000), pp 133-34.
7. Vincent, *Testaments*, p 195-96.
8. *Ibid*, p 209.
9. J A Hargreaves, 'Methodist growth and secession in the parish of Halifax, 1740-1851', *Transactions of the Halifax Antiquarian Society*, 7, 1999, pp 51-53.
10. B Wilson, Newspaper Articles, vol. 2, Horsfall Turner Collection, Calderdale Central Library; J A Hargreaves, '"Evangelical piety and Gallic flippancy": religion and popular protest in Halifax parish in the age of revolution' in K Dockray and K Laybourn, ed., *The Representation and Reality of War*, (Sutton, 1999), pp 75-77; E Yeo, 'Christianity in Chartist struggle 1838-1842', *Past and Present*, 91, 1981, pp 116-17.
11. Vincent, Testaments, pp 197-98.
12. Thompson, *The Chartists*, pp 293, 350; Vincent, Testaments, pp 198-203; Hargreaves, *Halifax*, pp 106-07; F C Mather, *Public Order in the age of the Chartists*, (Manchester University Press, 1959), pp 174-75.
13. Vincent, Testaments, pp 206-07, 210; F C Mather, *Chartism*, (Historical Association, 1965), cited in Wright, *Chartist Risings in Bradford*, p 2.
14. Vincent, *Testaments*, pp 210, 235.
15. Vincent, *Testaments*, pp 211-12.
16. Vincent, *Testaments*, pp 212, 233-37, 239; *Halifax Guardian*, 11 September 1885; Thompson, *The Chartists*, p 192; A Taylor, 'Commemoration, memorialisation and political memory in post-Chartist radicalism: the 1885 Halifax Chartist reunion in context' in O Ashton, R Fyson and S Roberts, eds, *The Chartist Legacy* (Merlin Press, 1999), pp 255-85.
17. W White, *Directory of the Clothing Districts of Yorkshire*, (Sheffield, 1853), p 686; Wilson, Newspaper Articles, vol. 2.
18. *Ibid*; Thompson, The Chartists, p 303; F C Mather, *Chartism and Society*, (Bell and Hyman, 1980), pp 110-11; M Blatchford, *The History of the Halifax Industrial Society*, (Halifax, 1901), pp 69-70.
19. Wilson, Newspaper Articles, vol. 1.
20. *Halifax Courier*, 22 June 1897; *Halifax Guardian*, 26 June 1897.
21. *Halifax Courier*, 3 July 1897; *Halifax Guardian*, 3 July 1897.

8. LADY BEHIND THE LENS: THE BACKGROUND TO THE ALICE LONGSTAFF GALLERY COLLECTION

by Issy Shannon

HEBDEN BRIDGE PHOTOGRAPHER ALICE LONGSTAFF (Figure 1) left behind two enduring legacies following her death, at the age of 84, in 1992.

The most important - and remarkable - is the vast collection of photographs and photographic artefacts which she accumulated and, fortunately for posterity, preserved, during a long career spanning an amazing seventy years.

The second legacy bequeathed by this most single-minded of ladies is a `mystery' - what was it that prompted a girl from an Upper Calder Valley farming family to opt, at the age of fourteen, to set her sights on the exotic, some might even say racy, world of photography?

At a time when most girls from her class and background were contemplating the relatively narrow and unexciting environs of a local textile mill or shop, the young Alice decided she wanted to be that still rare phenomenon - a lady photographer! But then Alice, as anyone who ever knew her will testify, was always a determined, strong-willed individual who, to the very end of her long and eventful life, `did it her way'.

re 1. Alice around the of her marriage in 1935. *ongstaff Gallery Collection (ALGC)*

Alice, née Speak, was born in 1907 and, together with her older brother Clement, brought up on the family farm, Little Learings, at Colden (Figure 2). In 1918, after attending the local primary school, she was awarded a County Minor Scholarship by the West Riding Education Committee, which included all tuition fees, cost of books, games equipment and - since she lived over two miles from Hebden Bridge United Secondary School where she had gained a place - travelling expenses too. The scholarship was for four years, to be

Figure 2. Little Lear Ings, Colden, as painted by Tom Whitehead. *ALGC*

renewed in 1922, but by then Alice had already left school to take up a life-long career in photography.

Alice's days at Hebden Bridge Grammar School (now Riverside Junior School) in Holme Street, came to an end in 1921, when she took up an apprenticeship with C Westerman: Photographer and Picture Framer. It may be no coincidence that their premises were just round the corner from the school, at West End, no doubt fascinating Alice from an early age and perhaps instrumental in inspiring her ambitions for the future. As was the custom of the day, Alice's parents paid a premium of £30, which was paid back at the princely rate of two shillings and sixpence a week (12.5p) over a three-year period as wages to the young apprentice.

The four Westerman daughters, chiefly Mrs Ada Redman, had continued running the businesses following their father's death in 1918, and in 1921 it was to the Hebden Bridge studio that fourteen-year-old Miss Alice Speak came as an eager apprentice.

She was extremely fortunate in that she had as her tutor and mentor Ada (Mrs Sydney Redman), thought by many to be the finest technician of the three photographers to run the business over its 100-year life. It was under Ada's expert tutelage that the young Alice learned all her skills and gained invaluable experience.

Ada ran the business until 1935, when she handed over the reins to her protege, by now adept and confident in every aspect of photography. Ada continued to live in retirement in Hebden Bridge until the age of 77; she died on 14 June 1961, at her home, 'Aigsgarth', on Birchcliffe Road.

By the time Alice took over the business she was a married woman and living with her husband, John Longstaff (Figure 3), next to the family farm at Little Learings Cottage. The couple were to remain there all their married life.

Legend has it that romance between Alice and John blossomed in the unlikely setting of bus journeys between Hebden Bridge and Burnley, which ran via Blackshaw Head near to Alice's home. John, from Bishop Auckland in North East England, had come to Halifax seeking work during the dark days of the Depression and was a conductor employed by the Hebble Bus Company on this route. The combination of his 'film-star' good looks and adroitness with the ticket machine obviously did the trick and the two were married in Nelson, Lancashire - hometown of

Figure 3. John's 'film-star' good looks were just the ticket as far as Alice was concerned. This studio portrait, c.1930s, was probably Alice's own work. *ALGC*

Figure 4. By the 1960s, 'C. Westerman - Photographer' had become 'Alice Longstaff - Photography - Pictures - Framing', but was still at the same premises in West End, Hebden Bridge. *ALGC*

Alice's mother - in 1935. For the first years of their married life John held a number of driving jobs with local firms, serving with the RAMC in India and Burma during the Second World War.

During this period Alice was assisted by her brother, Clement, who handled the developing and printing for the business. Formerly a weaver at Jack Bridge, Clement was well known as organist at Blakedean Chapel and was a member of Hebden Bridge Male Voice Choir. Following Clement's death John agreed to help out as picture framer; however Alice remained very much in charge and it was solely her name that appeared over the shop (Figure 4).

Over the years the premises - now Alice Longstaff Photography, Pictures and Framing (Figure 4) - had become something of a landmark in the town, serving as much as a 'drop-in centre', with the ever-sociable Alice always ready for a chat and a cuppa, as a retailer's.

A visit to the studio - in the yard at the back of the shop, now demolished (Figure 5) - was an established local tradition for a photo to mark every possible permutation of social event and family celebration. In fact it was almost a part of the wedding ceremony itself for newly-married couples to call at Alice's for the obligatory bridal portrait, before going on to the reception! It was these studio sittings above all that Alice loved, especially those involving children (Figures 6, 7 & 8). Many of her photographs were delicately hand-

Figure 5. The studio at the rear of Alice's shop. *Lloyd Greenwood*

Figure 6. One side of Alice's studio work. *ALGC*

Figure 7. A family composition by Alice. *ALGC*

Figure 8. Alice always had props available for her young sitters. *ALGC*

coloured by Alice herself; so meticulous was she that she took swatches of material from the clothing of the sitters, to be sure of capturing exactly the right shade.

Always a dedicated country-woman, Alice liked nothing better than to don comfortable tweeds and clogs and set off for a long walk over the moors around her beloved Colden Valley. Usually she was accompanied by one of the border or bearded collies she and John had all their lives – with, of course, a camera often in her hand.

It was one of her idiosyncrasies, however, that despite spending so much of her time behind the camera lens she was most reluctant to be in front of it and positively hated having her photo taken (Figure 9). Another of her personal aversions was an antipathy towards 'modern-day' contraptions such as TV and washing machines, which she refused to have in the house. To the end of her days her home was run pretty much according to the same housekeeping principles she had known in childhood.

She had no objection, though, to modern transport; in 1950 she amazed friends and family by taking an aeroplane trip with members

Figure 9. Alice and John pictured at one of the social functions they enjoyed in their later years. Alice appears highly amused, while John, true to character, is less easily amused! *ALGC*

Figure 10. Alice with members of the Hebden Bridge Literary & Scientific Society on their aerial photography trip. *ALGC*

of Hebden Bridge Literary and Scientific Society, taking aerial shots of the Calder Valley (Figure 10), and she and John were a familiar sight driving around the area in one of their large saloon cars. The couple often took elderly people on the car trips with them and were life-long supporters of the White Windows Cheshire Home in Sowerby Bridge, also involved with the Aged People's Welfare Committee and several other charities.

Indomitable to the end, Alice was entertaining friends at home and still working only a few days before her death in January 1992. She was just three months short of her 85th birthday and is buried in the garden of her old home at Little Learings, Colden. John returned to his native North East where he died, aged 89, in August 1999.

The Alice Longstaff Gallery Collection, which today comprises many thousands of photographs and photographic equipment dating as far back as the mid-1900s, is an invaluable legacy which lives on to mark the life and achievements of a truly remarkable and memorable lady.

The Alice Longstaff Gallery Collection is under the custodianship of trustees Frank and Beryl Woolrych, and Lloyd Greenwood, friends of Alice and John Longstaff for many years, and to them go my thanks for providing the illustrations for this brief article.

Figure 11. Alice at hay-making at Little Lear Ings. *Anon ALGC*

Crossley Westerman

A former fustian cutter born in Hebden Bridge in 1861, Crossley Westerman had seized the opportunity to turn a burgeoning hobby into a business and on the death of his mother took over her former toy shop, transforming it into a photographic studio which opened in 1892 (Figure 11).

By 1908 he was able to proudly boast that far from being a run-of-the-mill photographers, C Westerman was, in fact, an artistic 'Day and Electric Light Studio'. His lavish advert could not fail to impress and lure the customer seeking novelty and refinement: 'We have pleasure in reminding our customers of our thoroughly up-to-date and perfect system of artificial lighting by which photographs may be taken at night, in every respect equal to daylight pictures'. This benefit was in particular a great convenience, it continued, to 'ladies who desire to be photographed in evening or fancy dress, when attending a ball, bazaar or any such social function'.

So successful was this entrepreneurial photographer that he also established a studio at Victoria Road, Todmorden, in 1917, which he ran with his daughter Sarah. It was here, sadly, that Crossley Westerman met a sudden and somewhat tragic end on 25 August

Figure 11. Westerman's advert.

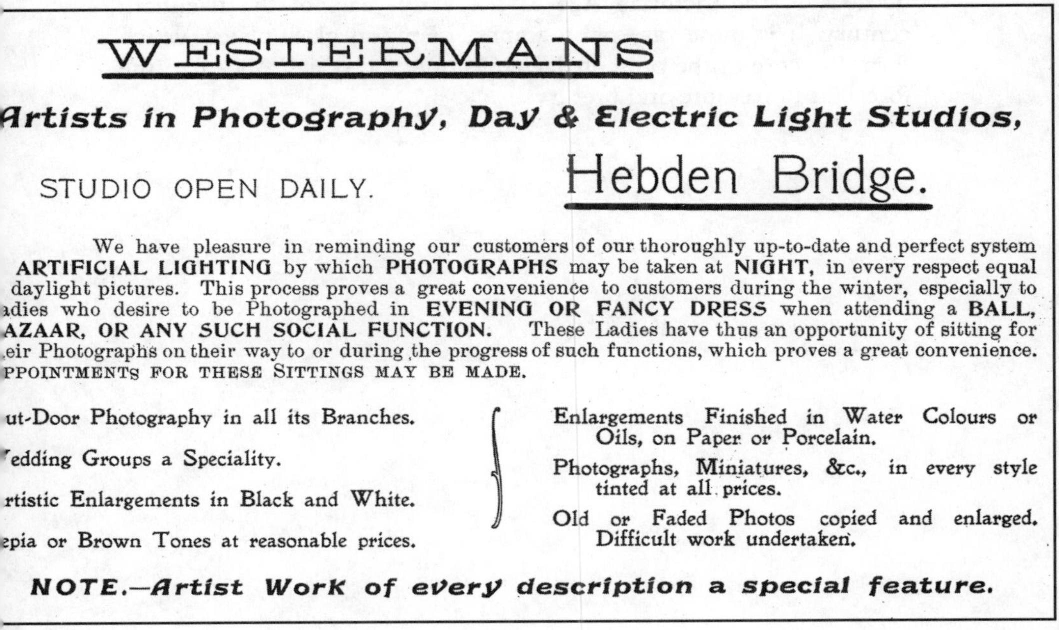

WESTERMANS

Artists in Photography, Day & Electric Light Studios,

STUDIO OPEN DAILY.   # Hebden Bridge.

We have pleasure in reminding our customers of our thoroughly up-to-date and perfect system ARTIFICIAL LIGHTING by which PHOTOGRAPHS may be taken at NIGHT, in every respect equal daylight pictures. This process proves a great convenience to customers during the winter, especially to ladies who desire to be Photographed in EVENING OR FANCY DRESS when attending a BALL, AZAAR, OR ANY SUCH SOCIAL FUNCTION. These Ladies have thus an opportunity of sitting for eir Photographs on their way to or during the progress of such functions, which proves a great convenience. PPOINTMENTS FOR THESE SITTINGS MAY BE MADE.

ut-Door Photography in all its Branches.

edding Groups a Speciality.

rtistic Enlargements in Black and White.

epia or Brown Tones at reasonable prices.

Enlargements Finished in Water Colours or Oils, on Paper or Porcelain.

Photographs, Miniatures, &c., in every style tinted at all prices.

Old or Faded Photos copied and enlarged. Difficult work undertaken.

NOTE.—Artist Work of every description a special feature.

1918, at the age of 57.

The *Hebden Bridge Times* captured the entire incident in a colourful obituary which nonetheless expressed all the esteem and affection in which he was held.

> He left his studio at Todmorden to catch the five o' clock train to Hebden Bridge...Having reached the end of Stansfield Road he was resting, as was his wont, when he had a sudden seizure.
>
> Dr Currie, of Riverside, being near at hand, was quickly on the scene, and from the fact that he had lately been consulted by Mr Westerman was conversant with the patient. Meanwhile Mr Westerman had completely collapsed and passed away, and all that the doctor could do was pronounce life extinct.
>
> The body was afterwards reverently removed to the public mortuary at Waterside.

Paying tribute to a highly popular man the *HBT* concluded: 'Mr Westerman had been in business as a photographer for 27 years, establishing two successful businesses with the help of his daughters. In social life he was equally well known, being invariably genial and hearty and proving acceptable company.'

More than anyone else Crossley Westerman was responsible for recording on camera scenes of the Hebden Bridge area, from the last decades of the Victorian Age to the early years of the twentieth century. It is these rare photographs, many on glass plates, which form the core of the present-day collection and which Alice had the foresight to treasure and preserve.

9. THE WARLEY MAYPOLE

by Garry Stringfellow

FOR MANY, THE WARLEY MAYPOLE will conjure up an image of the long-established public house of that name standing close by the fountain and lamp at the heart of Warley town. C H Tordoff, however, in his account of the township of Warley, *The Warley Story*, tells us that in 1773 it was in the ownership of Joseph Farrar and then known as *The Horns*. It is not uncommon for such establishments to undergo a change of name and this almost certainly happened here sometime early in the first half of the nineteenth century, following the erection of a maypole close by.[1]

The earliest reference that I have yet found to this maypole is from the *Halifax Courier* of 1 August 1863, when it reported that a number of 'influential gentlemen' were determined to erect a new pole to commemorate the visit to Halifax of the Prince and Princess of Wales. The report opened with a reference to earlier maypoles:

> *In the year 1814, when peace was declared between England and France, the inhabitants of Warley erected a Maypole in the centre of Warley-town in commemoration thereof. It remained there for a number of years, and was ultimately blown down.*
>
> *A second one was erected, which was taken down a number of years since* [2]

The article does not give the source of the information, but later reports suggest that it was still remembered by the older generation. If this was the case, then as often happens, the memory of one may be questioned by another, for an article in the *Halifax Courier* for 1882 stated that.

> *The first was erected to commemorate the victory at Waterloo in 1815.*[3]

The battle of Waterloo took place on 18 June and to erect a maypole after this date would appear to be a curious thing to do, it being too late for a joint victory and May celebration. On 6 April 1814, however, Napoleon abdicated for the first time and on 11 April the Treaty of Fontainbleu was signed, both good reasons for a celebration, with time to erect a pole and to organise celebrations before May Day. There are no details of those early festivities and it is not until 1863 that we are treated to the most interesting accounts of the doings of those 'influential gentlemen' of Warley, their supporters and their opponents.

The first reported meeting of those responsible for erecting the mid-Victorian maypole was on 16 August 1863 at the *Maypole Inn*, when those present were William Dearden, of Warley Grammar School; William Bowers; William Radcliffe, tailor of Warley Town Lane, William Dixon, watchmaker of Sowerby Bridge and John Levers, of Steps. Later additions to the committee were Joseph Sutcliffe, woolsorter of Warley Town Lane, and John Taylor, tailor and draper of Marsh.[4]

Their initial intention to erect the pole to coincide with the Royal visit was thwarted, because the approval of the local authorities had to be sought and their next meeting was not until after the Royal visit. On 12 August, however, the Warley Local Board resolved that...

> ... *leave be given to the subscribers, to erect a May Pole in the centre of the space in Warley Town, provided that a gas lamp be affixed thereto.*[5]

The Mayor and Town Clerk of Luddenden were invited to take part in the inaugural proceedings, but it appears that many of the townships' worthies were kept in the dark about their plans until they appeared in the local news.

Opposition started to mount and in the *Halifax Guardian* of 3 October the first of a series of letters of opposition appeared.

> *THE MAYPOLE. — To the Editor of the Halifax Guardian. — Sir,— Permit me through your paper to address a few words to the inhabitants of Warley respecting the proposed erection of a maypole in that village. Some old customs and institutions are worth preserving, some it is as well to let die, among the latter I venture to think is the maypole of Warley.*

Perhaps for some of the locals, the activities associated with previous poles were not to their liking. We are left to speculate on the reasons for this correspondent's opposition. The letter continues ...

> *I have made considerable enquiries and am unable to find out who are the promoters of the affair, but I know this, there is a very general disapproval of the project on the part of those who usually take the lead in our village matters.*

The writer of the letter thinks that a maypole is an inappropriate way of celebrating a Royal visit, the only person to benefit will be the innkeeper, and goes on to suggest that ..

> *A much better plan it seems to me, would be to make a modest fountain in the centre of the open space in front of the chapel, and combine it with a public lamp, capable of lighting up the three roads which there meet.*

The letter is signed – ONE OF THEMSELVES.[6]

This particular 'ONE' clearly believed that plans for the pole had been made covertly, something that the organising committee vehemently denied in the next issue of the newspaper.

> *To the Editor of the Halifax Guardian, – Sir, – in reply to your May Pole correspondent, who, I feel assured, must be some old woman, whose taste for that which is beautiful and harmless is evidently on the decline, ...* [7]

The letter goes on to bring to her (?) attention the announcement of their intentions that had appeared in the *Halifax Courier* of 1 August. But feelings were mixed on the matter and on the previous Thursday, following 'the Fair', when it was customary to have a public tea-party

> *... Not a single ticket was sold, consequently not a single cup of tea was made. The reason is said to be in consequence of the present unpleasantness respecting the Maypole; the proposed erection of which has not met with the approbation of so many of the inhabitants as was first expected.* [8]

The fair, which took place at Warley on the Wednesday preceding this report, was primarily for the sale of livestock, but swinging boats, nut stalls and other shows also appear to have been an integral part of the annual event.

Objections were also voiced in the *Halifax Courier* of the same week and in the *Guardian* again the following week, but the 'committee' were men of action and by the end of the month both papers were reporting on the arrival and erection of the pole.

WARLEY.

> *MAY POLE, – On Tuesday the finial or heraldic device for the top of the May pole, arrived in Warley. It was taken to the May Pole Inn, where hundreds availed themselves of the opportunity of seeing it. The unanimous opinion was that it was a splendid piece of workmanship, and that it was to be regretted that it should be placed*

Figure 1. The maypole in the late 1890s.
Photograph restored by Peter Allsopp

so high up where its beautiful qualities could not be so minutely ascertained. On Wednesday the ornamental gallery arrived, a piece of craft which does credit to Mr. Wm. Birch, of Halifax. It is of the circular form, and made to imitate a fruit basket. The finial and the gallery were fixed to the May Pole, and a hole was made six feet deep, of which one foot eight inches is rock. [9]

The finial, which represented fruit, acorns and leaves, was carved by Mr Hellawell, of Gibbet Street, and a photograph of the pole taken late in the century suggests that the finial was about five feet high (Figure 1).

The erection of the pole was entrusted to John Henry Turner, of Winterburn-hill, but when attempts were made to raise it, they had to be abandoned because of the inadequacy of the tackle. On the following day, however ...

... On Thursday after the tackle had been adjusted to the May Pole, in a few minutes it was wound up with the most perfect ease and placed in position amid the cheering of some of the most powerful voices that it has been our pleasure to hear for a long time. [10]

William Garnett had been appointed to execute a design. Made from Norwegian pine, painted blue, black and white, the erected pole must have been an impressive sight. Standing 69 feet 6 inches (21.2m.) high, its diameter at the base was 19½ inches (0.5m.), tapering to six inches at the top.

Still the opposition continued and it was not restricted to village residents. The trustees of the United Reform Chapel wrote to the Local Board, but at their next meeting on 11 November the Board decided not to interfere with arrangements, as it already been erected with their approval.

The inaugural dinner was held at the *May Pole Inn* on the evening of 25 November. The pole was decorated with flags and evergreens and a display of gas illuminations were set up. Regrettably, the pipe supplying them was too small and only sufficient to light up the Prince of Wales plumes and the initials V R. Nevertheless ...

... From all round the people assembled; throughout the evening

crowds surrounded the pole, singing and dancing at intervals, and enlivened by the performances of Warley amateur band.[11]

Whilst this was the scene outside, in the public house ...

... The dinner was all that could be wished, and that being over, The chairman gave the usual toast. A party of the Halifax Glee and Madrigal Society sang the National Anthem, and 'God bless the Prince of Wales', followed by appropriate songs at intervals throughout the evening. Sergeant Leevers of the Sowerby Bridge volunteers suitably responded to the toast of 'the Army and Navy.'[12]

William Dearden, local poet and chairman of the committee, spoke at some length on the history of maypoles and Mr Bowers, the secretary, gave a financial statement to the effect that the expenditure of the committee was £32 and subscriptions were only £22. At this point in the proceedings we may assume that all were feeling extremely agreeable, for when an additional round of subscriptions were asked for, the subscribers were so generous that the surplus was sufficient to provide a tea party for the 'women of the neighbourhood'. There were numerous toasts and 'the company did not break up until a late hour'.

The subscriptions came from a variety of sources, some of them being among the most eminent and affluent gentlemen of the area. They included Sir Henry Edwards, MP, and Captain Edwards; James Green, woollen manufacturer of Sowerby Bridge; Richard Wood, iron founder of Sowerby Bridge; James Oldfield of Warley House; John Naylor, brewer of Warley; Messrs James Clay and Sons of Sowerby Bridge and Michael Stocks, brewer.

The organising committee, having achieved their first goal, now had to wait until the following year to see how people would respond to an opportunity to celebrate May Day with the new pole as the focus of attention. They could not have been disappointed. The *Halifax Courier* described the village as having a 'holiday appearance with every house having its number of visitors'. The *Halifax Guardian* reported ...

WARLEY.

THE MAY POLE. - In honour of the advent of spring, the recently erected May-pole, on Monday last, was decorated with sundry flags, streamers, and garlands, and presented a very gay appearance. The Warley brass band also paraded, and gave the village a very lively aspect. It is computed that between 2,000 and 3,000 persons visited

the usually quiet little village. Such was the crush, that the large lodge-
room at the inn, where some addresses had intended to have been
delivered, was crowded out with thirsty customers, and the speeches
consequently had to be omitted. One address, however, was given by
the secretary to the committee for erecting the May-pole, who expressed
his regret that the ancient custom of dancing around a May-pole had,
along with other pastimes , ceased to exist. [13]

It is curious to note that the relatively new fashion at that time, of
plaiting ribbons round the lower half of a maypole, was not adopted
at Warley, not in 1864, nor in subsequent years as far as I can
ascertain. Descriptions of the dancing that took place around
maypoles in England prior to the 1850s are vague, but during the
second half of the nineteenth century maypole dancing with ribbons
became part of the repertoire of ballet and other dance masters, as
the attempt to revive the essence of 'Merrie England' became a
popular activity.[14] As ribbons are not mentioned in any report, we
may assume that the dancing briefly referred to in later descriptions
of the events were the popular social dances of the day, and therefore
not worth reporting in detail.

The popularity of the celebrations increased over the following
years and by the end of the decade the number of those attending
was estimated at between 4,000 and 5,000.

In 1867, the *Halifax Courier* reported ...

WARLEY.

MAY DAY.- Wednesday being May-Day the villagers were astir. The
May-pole wore its usual honours, being decorated with flags,
evergreens, and banners. The weather being very fine during the
evening, a very large number of persons assembled and the 'old, old
tale' must have been very often repeated, judging by the numerous
lovers who were present. The 'Warley amateurs' discoursed sweet
music, and it was not till long after old Sol had sunk behind the
western hills that the majority of the company appeared to think of
wending their way homeward, dancing and other amusements being
kept up until a late hour. [15]

In 1872 the landlady of the *Maypole Inn* was ill and the celebrations
were allowed to lapse. She was again unwell the following year and
died in the early summer, but in 1874 the event was revived and the
pole repainted by Levi Crabtree of Luddenden, the upper half white,
the lower half blue.

Some of the best descriptions of the celebrations are from the newspapers of 1878 and 1879, when they described activities that the village is unlikely to have seen since that time.

... There floated at the top a beautiful streamer, 30 feet long, and the gallery, which is about the middle of the pole, was filled with Union Jacks, banners, &c. Underneath the gallery was filled with flowers. Shortly after three o'clock the Friendly Brass Band put in its appearance, and opened its programme by playing 'May Day', after which dancing commenced, and continued (with short intervals) until nine o'clock. At this time the crowd was very large, and it was computed that about 3000 people were present. A number of soldiers from the Depot gave a very nice appearance to the crowd. There were swinging boats, cross-bow shooting, Aunt Sally and 'all the fun of the fair', together with oyster and other stalls. [16]

...The 'ancient festivities' consisted of dancing to the music of the Friendly Brass Band. As evening came on, the visitors from Halifax and Sowerby Bridge were very numerous. Among the latter were some worthies who entered the village bearing a flag and curious musical instruments. They left, or some of them, bearing the same flag, also a refreshing quantity of malt liquor. The May Pole Inn was crowded with customers, and the outside refreshments of various kinds were dispensed from stalls. At one shop the announcement was seen 'sandwiges' sold 'hear', much to the surprise, it is conjectured, of the officials of the School Board. [17]

The event however did not pass without incident and the *Sowerby Bridge Chronicle* of 1885 reported...

AT THE MAY POLE a young man named Henry Smith, labourer of Tuel Lane, Sowerby Bridge, was brought up at the West Riding Police Court, Halifax, on Saturday. Superintendent Carr said the defendant was locked up on the previous night for damaging a stall at Warley. It was the feast and there was dancing round the Maypole and the defendant and others acted rather foolishly. The defendant expressed his regret for what he had done. The case was settled on his paying the amount of damages 7/6d (37.5p).

The last description of Mayday in Warley in the Halifax newspapers was in 1885, when it was still drawing large crowds.

The failure of local newspapers to report on Warley Mayday celebrations is not, however, evidence for its discontinuation; references to Mayday in general became infrequent, even though the parades of decorated horses of the local manufacturers continued well into the twentieth century. The condition of the pole, however, deteriorated, and by 1888 its condition was such that a replacement was the only solution if the village was not to lose its most prominent feature.

> *WARLEY LOCAL BOARD. In Warley Town a deputation from the chapel trustees, consisting of the Rev T Whitely, and Mr Tom Sutcliffe, met the Board to urge the desirability of setting a portion of the road near the chapel, and also to complain about the condition of the Maypole. Upon examination the pole was found to be decayed and unless the parties interested put the pole into safe condition the Board will doubtless have to take measures, to protect the lives and property of the rate payers from any injury which might follow its fall during a gale.*[18]

Following this letter, a committee was formed with the aim of replacing the pole. The new pole was shorter and stouter, but reports give no further details other than to say that it was not painted.

It seems strange that the activities which took place up until 1885 and possibly until 1888, ceased when the old pole was taken down. In 1890 the *Halifax Courier* reported

> *MAY DAY has gone without any public ceremonial around the May Pole. The pole has not yet been painted and decorated, which is one reason for the omission of the May Day celebrations.*

Perhaps the organisers were getting old and out of touch with the younger generation who may have made up the greater part of the revellers.

Over the following years the pole must have taken on a rather forlorn appearance, its fabric deteriorating with the years, until the winter of 1898/9 when it was blown down. There appears to have been little damage done other than to the railings that surrounded it. In February that winter, the District Council instructed the surveyor to remove the railings and the stones that occupied the site.[19] Nine weeks later the *Halifax Guardian* reported...

> *A GIFT OF A DRINKING FOUNTAIN. Mr A S McCrea of Warley House has informed the district council that he is about to present to the district a trough, lamp and drinking fountain, made of the best native stone and wrought iron, to be erected on the site of the Maypole, at Warley Town. The Council tendered their thanks to the donor at their meeting on Monday.*[20]

In October the fountain was formally handed over to the district by

Figure 2. The fountain. Photograph taken in the early part of the twentieth century.

Mr McCrea and although the newspapers reported that 'the brief proceedings were of an interesting nature',[21] we are not enlightened further.

It took thirty-seven years, almost to the month, before a fountain was erected following the suggestion made in the *Halifax Guardian* made by 'ONE OF THEMSELVES' - it would be interesting to know if he or she lived to see it (Figure 2).

Other Maypoles in Calderdale.

Having described at some length the happenings around the Warley Maypole, it would seem appropriate to make some reference to other maypoles in Calderdale and in doing so a very brief history of maypoles in general would also seem appropriate.

In Europe there are references to maypoles reaching back to Roman times and it has been suggested that they may be linked to the festival of Floralia c.239 BC. It is certain that they were widespread throughout Europe by the eighth century.

Records show that Mayday celebrations in England were popular with some classes of society but viewed as ungodly riotous affairs by others; nevertheless they continued in many parts of the country up until the Commonwealth period when Parliament in 1644 ordered that they should be taken down.

In Halifax the maypole stood at the corner of Corn Market and Old Market until about 1630. We learn this from the diary of Oliver Heywood, who in 1680 described the riotous Mayday celebrations then taking place in the town and goes on to reflect on times past, when

> there was never such work in Halifax above fifty years past, at which time Dr Favour was Vicar, Mr John Barlow Lecturer, at that time rude people brought in a maypole, but they strenuously opposed them in preaching, but all hell broke loose. [22]

In the years following the restoration of the monarchy, Mayday celebrations were revived along with other customs and were seen by many as a return to the fun and games of an idealised Elizabethan Merrie England'. During the nineteenth century more maypoles were erected throughout the country in association with mock pageants, a popular event of the time.

According to one Mr Baldwin, a maypole stood at the junction of New Street and Deep Lane in Clifton. The pole probably stood until the 1870s.[23] Also, the great grandmother of J Horsfall Turner could remember a serious encounter between the youths of Rastrick and Brighouse because the latter had stolen the Rastrick maypole. This was probably in the early nineteenth century.[24]

The only other reference I have found to a maypole in Calderdale is one erected at the *Shibden Mill Inn*. It is likely that the proprietor of that establishment had witnessed the popular celebrations in Warley and decided to take a piece of the action for himself.

Figure 3. The *Maypole Inn* in 1992. *John Billingsley*

SHIBDEN.

THE MAYPOLE - To give this, the Queen of months, welcome, a Maypole has been erected at the Shibden Mill Inn, and on Monday it was the means of drawing together many visitors from the town and neighbourhood. A band was in attendance, and dancing round the pole, &c., was kept up till late in the evening. The farmers in this peaceful valley would all be glad to see so many visitors to look at the beauties of nature; but their joy is generally turned to grief when they find that these visitors have knocked a great many of their fences and walls down.[25]

The *Halifax Guardian* records these celebrations at Shibden up until 1883, and whilst it is possible that they may have continued past this date, it is likely that as with Warley the residents were finding other interests to take their place.

Notes and References

1. *Walker's Halifax Directory.* J U Walker, 1845.
2. *Halifax Courier* 1 August 1863.
3. *Halifax Courier* 6 May 1882.
4. *Halifax Courier* 6 May 1882.
5. *Transactions of the Warley Local Board* August 1863.
6. *Halifax Guardian* 3 October 1863.
7. *Halifax Guardian* 10 October 1863.
8. *Halifax Guardian* 10 October 1863.
9. *Halifax Courier* 31 October 1863.
10. *Halifax Courier* 31 October 1863.
11. *Halifax Courier* 28 November 1863.
12. *Halifax Courier* 28 November 1863.
13. *Halifax Guardian* 7 May 1864.
14. Roy Judge. *Proceedings of the Second Traditional Dance Conference.* Crewe & Alsager College of Higher Education 1982.
15. *Halifax Courier* 4 May 1867.
16. *Halifax Guardian* 4 May 1878.
17. *Halifax Courier* 3 May 1879.
18. *Halifax Courier* 2 June 1888.
19. *Halifax Guardian* 27 February 1899.
20. *Halifax Guardian* 5 May 1900.
21. *Halifax Guardian* 27 October 1900.
22. J Horsfall Turner. *Rev Oliver Heywood BA. His Autobiography, Diaries, Anecdotes and Events Book.* 1882.
23. H N & M Pobjoy. *The Story of the Ancient Parish of Hartshead cum Clifton.* 1972.
24. J Horsfall Turner. *Our Customary Feasts.* Reprints for the *Brighouse Echo,* 1913.
25. *Halifax Guardian* 4 May 1871.

10. FROM QUILL TO COMPUTER: PUBLIC LIBRARIES IN HALIFAX

by Derek Bridge

THERE WERE NUMEROUS LIBRARIES in the ancient world with collections of scrolls and papyri, notably at Pergamum, Antioch, and the great library at Alexandria where scholars gathered, in addition to a number scattered about Greece itself. Egypt and China too, were known for their libraries and for their learning, and the Greek trend was followed later by the Romans who combined the library with baths and sporting facilities. However, the present-day public library may be considered to have its genesis in the parochial libraries set up in England during the sixteenth and seventeenth centuries.

In Halifax, the Parish Church of St John the Baptist had a library which was instituted by Dr Robert Clay, Vicar of Halifax 1624-28,[1] a friend and follower of Sir Thomas Bodley, whose own interest in libraries was demonstrated in his founding of the Oxford University Library which bears his name. A crypt, or charnel house, was cleared of bones and the new library set up. In the Churchwardens' Accounts appears the gruesome entry: 'paid for dressing both Revestry and carrying out the bones, 4s'.[2] This fine collection included some incunabula and the books were chained to the shelves as in Hereford Cathedral. Among the more valuable books was a black-letter copy of the *Old Testament* in two volumes, printed in Nuremberg in 1481 by the famous Anthon Koburger with hand-coloured woodcuts and illuminated capitals.

The chains were removed in 1710 but the cold, damp atmosphere of the crypt took its toll and the fine calf bindings were ruined, showing traces of verdigris, while foxing discoloured many pages, and when the collection was examined by an expert in 1957 none of the books had been rebound for a hundred years. In 1966 the collection of some 247 books, of which no fewer than 231 were printed before 1645,[3] were transferred to York University, where they were restored or rebound and shelved in a dry room at an even temperature where the humidity could be controlled.

A later development was the formation of the Halifax Circulation Library, which started in a first floor room in the Old Cock Yard in

Figure 1: The Assembly Rooms, Harrison Road; the original location of Halifax Public Library. *Calderdale Libraries.*

1767 and was moved in 1818 to rooms near the Theatre Royal,[4] finally being transferred to the New Assembly Rooms on Harrison Road (Figure 1), which were built on the site later to be occupied by the Police Headquarters and the Magistrates Courts. By 1836 the library consisted of 7,000 volumes. The Luddenden Library was established in 1781 at the *Lord Nelson Inn*, where it was used by Branwell Bronte while employed at Luddenden Foot Station. The remaining volumes of this collection are now kept in Calderdale Central Library. For the more affluent there was the Halifax Subscription Library which charged a membership fee of five guineas (£5.25) in 1804, a cost which put it far beyond the reach of the ordinary working person, but despite the expense there were nearly 200 subscribers by 1814.[5]

In the building known as Scarborough Castle,[6] which stood in Crown Street, was a private newspaper room recorded in 1809 and run by Mr B Milnes. Another library, run by Thomas Gledhill, which was described as a public library, originated in a meeting of the Dissenters and was opened in 1823 in the Old Cock Yard five years after the Circulation Library had moved from there. A small Subscription Library, mainly fiction, consisting of some 4,600 volumes, was maintained in Waterhouse Street in 1848.[7]

The first library in Halifax which may be regarded as intended for the use and education of the working man was in the Mechanics Institute, inaugurated in 1825 at Woolshops. This was later moved to Horton Street and subsequently amalgamated with a Reading Room which had been established in a house in Wesley Court in 1847, before coming to its final home in Crossley Street in the building known as the Marlborough Hall. By 1874 the Mechanics' Institute had 1,272 members and a library of 8,000 volumes, which were issued at the rate of 22,433 per year.[8] Five years after the establishment of the Mechanics' Institute, the Halifax Literary and Philosophical Society was formed in 1830 with its own museum and library. The society was at first located in rooms adjoining those of the Halifax Circulating Library and rented from the proprietors of the New Assembly Rooms. New premises were built on Harrison Road in 1836 and an extension made for the library, which amalgamated with the Circulating library in 1865-66.[9]

Colonel Edward Akroyd, the local industrialist and philanthropist, was instrumental in founding a library with several thousand books for his workpeople in connection with the Haley Hill Institution, which was an educational organisation similar to the one which he founded at Copley village, two miles to the south of Halifax, in 1850. The library of the Haley Hill Institution was overhauled in 1856 and new additions made, bringing the total stock to 3,000, and by 1864 membership had grown to 300.[10] The Copley Library was contained in one of the classrooms in the school and for thirteen years was free to the employees of James Akroyd and Son. It is significant that after some improvements were carried out in 1863, and a small charge was made, the membership quickly dropped from 200 to 30.[11]

A similar library was provided by the firm of John Crossley and Sons Ltd at the Dean Clough Institute, built and furnished by them for their employees, and containing lending and reference libraries, a reading room, a large lecture and concert hall and billiards rooms.[12] Other libraries of the time were the Northowram Institute,[13] which commenced in 1852, the Halifax Church Institute, founded in 1858, and the Halifax Co-operative Society in 1873. When this last was discontinued, the library of over 4,000 books was sold to Halifax

Corporation for £250 and incorporated in the stock of Halifax Municipal Library when it was organised in 1881.[14]

This will serve to give some idea of the local interest in books and reading and of the available sources of book loans in Halifax, particularly in the nineteenth century. None of these brought books within the reach of everyone. The subscription libraries were much too expensive for the ordinary working man, who in most cases found it hard to buy the necessities of life, and the other libraries which were available catered only for certain sections of the community. As we have already seen the libraries which were available free were quite well used, considering the general state of literacy, but when a small charge was made membership plummeted, a clear pointer that there was a strong need for a free library available to all.

The first *Public Libraries Act* of 1850 provided for libraries to be run by local authorities from the proceeds of a penny rate, but town councils were slow to avail themselves of this opportunity, many councillors being undecided as to whether such a step would be beneficial to all concerned. The first move in Halifax was on 17 November 1866, when Joseph Atkins, secretary of the Halifax Trades Council, sent a letter to the Mayor of Halifax petitioning for a free library in the town.[15] No action was taken as a result of this, and it was not until 1881 that the matter was raised again, this time by Alderman J W Davis, whose letter to the *Halifax Courier* on 19 March 1881[16] set out the advantages of a public library and stated the case for one in Halifax. The town meeting which this prompted led to the adoption of the *Public Libraries Act*, and although this was thirty-one years after the Act was passed Halifax was still only the 87th authority to do so.

The first Libraries Committee included Alderman Davis, Louis J Crossley, John Lister, the Reverend J Bryan Dale and the vicar, the Reverend F Pigou.[17] There was considerable difficulty in finding a suitable site for the library. Various schemes for the erection of a new building were considered and attempts were made to join with other institutions in the town. Overtures were made to the Mechanics Institute with the object of purchasing or otherwise transferring the library of that society to the Public Library Committee and occupying the large hall of the Mechanics Institute as a free library and newsroom.[18] The final choice, however, rested between the Assembly Rooms on Harrison Road and the Odd Fellows Hall on St James Road. Strangely enough, the Odd Fellows Hall, or Halifax Trades Club as it later came to be called, was again considered for conversion into a Central Library in 1954. On both occasions the idea was rejected and in 1882 the Assembly Rooms were chosen at a rental of £120 per annum.[19]

A well-stocked public newsroom was opened on 20 March 1882,[20] which from the start proved very popular, being used by an average of a thousand people a day. The first Librarian, Joseph Reed Welch, of South Shields, had been appointed in January[21] at a salary of £80 per annum with two assistants at ten shillings (50p) a week. A temporary cataloguer was engaged at the relatively enormous sum of £3 10s (£3.50) a week, and by August it was found necessary to appoint two special assistants at 25 shillings (£1.25) a week to help with the cataloguing.

A hundred chairs were ordered at 7s 6d (37.5p) each, with ten American walnut tables at £3 5s (£3.25) each,[22] and the original estimate for books was £2,000. It is symptomatic of the times that the Binding Committee proposed that books should be bound in Persian Morocco. This has a beautiful appearance and is soft and pliable, but the industrial atmosphere of nineteenth-century Halifax, with its high level of soot content and sulphur fumes, proved much too corrosive for any form of leather binding unless specially treated.

After careful consideration it was decided to use bookcases similar to those at Bradford Municipal Library. These were free-standing and could easily be moved should the library be transferred to another location. Twenty of these were purchased, each capable of holding a thousand volumes. The problem of acquiring sufficient books at a reasonable cost was helped to some extent by a number of local organisations offering their own libraries at a low cost.

A small anteroom was shelved, and furnished with books for the use of children, the furniture, as throughout the library, being of walnut, and it was decided to print 3,000 copies of the catalogue, to be produced in separate parts as the stock was processed. By January 1883 the first part of the Lending Library, consisting of 7,000 volumes of fiction and children's literature, was available to borrowers and shortly afterwards the remainder of the library was completed with a stock of about 25,000 books.

In the early days the Reference Library was open from 10 am until 10 pm, and the Lending Library until 9 pm. No-one under the age of sixteen was allowed in the Reference Library, and the use of ink was prohibited - this last rule is one which still applies in the Archives Department. Each year the library was closed for stocktaking during the first two weeks of July.[23]

A policeman was on duty each evening at the library entrance[24] to regulate the large crowds and to prevent damage, for vandalism is not solely a manifestation of the late twentieth century. The Library Minutes of June 1883 record a resolution:

> that the Town Clerk be requested to write to the Head Master and Mistress of the higher Board School drawing their attention to the misbehaviour of a number of boys and girls from the school in the entrance and vestibule of the library, and requesting their influence in endeavouring to suppress such misbehaviour

There was also a case of writing on the wall of the vestibule, but in this instance, 'the moving finger having writ,' as Omar Khayyam put it, moved on too slowly and the culprit was 'brought to book'. The wall was repainted and charged to the account of the offender.[25]

The Penny Rate, which was levied on 1 January 1882, produced an income of £1,050 and the Committee decided to augment this income with a loan of £2,000[26] to be repaid over ten years. A few months later it was found that this sum would be inadequate to meet their requirements and the loan was increased by a further £1,000, making a total capital sum of £4,050. During the first twelve months the expenditure incurred by the Committee in setting up, furnishing, and stocking the library amounted to £3,756 3s 3d (£3,756.16p).

Within a few years it became necessary to provide for readers living at the east and northern side of town, and in 1887 Bankfield, the former residence of Colonel Edward Akroyd, was purchased by Halifax Corporation for the nominal sum of £6,000 and adapted for a branch library, museum and art gallery.[27] The sum of £1,000 was borrowed, repayable over fifteen years, but the cost of adapting the premises for library use and supplying furniture and books amounted to £1,949. About 12,000 volumes were bought for stock and the Patents Library, formerly housed in the Town Hall, was transferred to the new branch. Joseph Whiteley was engaged to catalogue the books, and after the library opened on 8 August 1888 he was appointed Branch Librarian.

Whiteley's assistant was L S Iastrzebski, better known as Stanley Jast, who later became a prominent figure in the library world. Jast was the son of a European émigré living in Halifax and worked with Halifax Libraries for some years before moving on and achieving fame. He was appointed assistant librarian in 1888 when Joseph Whiteley became Librarian, and subsequently became Branch Librarian at Akroyd. When Jast resigned in 1892 Edward Green, who was Sub-Librarian at Belle Vue, was appointed to fill the post.[28]

The popularity of the Central Library brought problems in its wake. The size of the room was totally inadequate for the number of readers, who frequently had to wait for a seat. Within a month of opening there were 2,676 readers registered and 7,329 volumes had been borrowed - a daily average of 305 volumes. It was stated in the Annual Report that the Reference Library suffered from want of space, not only for the books but also for the readers. This was a complaint which was to re-echo down the years.[29] The Annual Report for 1885-6 stated with regard to the Newsroom:

> *The pressure in the evening is very great, and a serious want of accommodation is of daily occurrence. If the space available for readers were double or treble that now provided, the Committee has no hesitation in saying that it would not be excessive and that every seat would be taken.*

This lack of space applied equally to the Lending Department, for on a Saturday evening between 800 and 1,000 books were usually exchanged in the limited area by the indicators.[30]

In 1889 Belle Vue was bought by the Corporation for £8,000,[31] which was a purely nominal sum in view of the expense incurred by the former owner, Sir Francis Crossley, in building and land costs. It was here that Lord Somerleyton, Sir Francis's son, had been born. After some structural alterations had been carried out, the library was transferred from the Assembly Rooms to its new home where it opened in September 1890 (Figures 2 & 3). Joseph Whiteley was now Librarian, having been promoted from Branch Librarian at Akroyd Branch in 1889 when J Reed Welch resigned.

During the early years Halifax Municipal Libraries were conducted on the 'indicator' system, by which a borrower had first

Figure 2. Belle Vue, c. 1890; the second home of Halifax Public Library. *Calderdale Libraries*

Figure 3. Staircase at Belle Vue decorated for the visit of the Duke of York, 1896. *Calderdale Libraries.*

to consult the catalogue to find the number of the book required, then refer to the large indicator boards to see if the corresponding number registered 'in,' and finally quote the number to the assistant at the counter. This was known as a 'closed access' system, as all books had to be obtained from the assistant and the public had no access to the shelves.

Mr Whiteley attended the Annual Meeting of the Library Association in 1891 and commented on a paper entitled 'Fines for the damage of books'. He was much concerned about the problem of readers writing in the margins or mutilating books. This always seems to have been the public librarian's *bête noir*. The Minutes of September 1897 contain a resolution that the loss of Watson's *History of Halifax* be advertised in the Halifax papers and a reward of £1 be offered for its recovery.

In 1894 sub-branch libraries were opened in the Board Schools at Mixenden, Bradshaw and Siddal[32] with teachers engaged as Sub-Librarians, and a branch was opened in Moorside School in 1895.

The Librarian's report for 1902 contained the following statement:

> *I question very much whether any other town in the kingdom is so well off in having such an admirably situated building, standing as it does, in its own grounds, away from the noise and turmoil of the streets, and at the same time, not more than three minutes walk from two of the principal tram routes.*

While one applauds Mr Whiteley's sentiments with regard to the siting of the library from an aesthetic point of view, it is questionable whether a Central Library which is a tram ride from the town centre is well-situated. A library which is away from the 'turmoil of the streets' is also away from the majority of the reading public, and for many years there was an obvious need for a new Central Library which was not only designed and built as a library, but also situated in the town centre.

In September 1906 Joseph Whiteley was replaced as Librarian by Edward Green,[33] who began to re-organise both libraries, completely replacing the indicator system at Bankfield by a scheme of close classification, and borrowers were allowed direct access to the shelves. This proved so successful that the same methods were applied at the Central Library where the changes were more extensive. Until 1906 the Lending and Reference Libraries had been housed in a communicating suite of rooms running all down the south side of the building and part way along the western side. The Reading Room was situated in a great, lofty room on the northern side of the building. The changes of 1906 led to a complete reversal of this arrangement; the large room to the north now became the Lending Library, and the rooms on the south side were adapted for use as a Reference Library and Reading Rooms.

These various alterations, together with the publication of a reader's quarterly guide, the issue of special non-fiction tickets and the institution of informal 'Talks about Books', resulted in a greatly increased circulation and the wider use of the more serious classes of books. The Chairman of the Libraries Committee was authorised to obtain two or three specimens of book-binding by the Edwards family, notable Halifax binders of the early nineteenth century. Book-binding tools and leather were also bought so that books could be rebound on the premises.

In April 1917 Greenroyd Lodge was taken over for use as a branch library at Skircoat. This served the area until 1 October 1926 when a purpose-built library was opened, a pleasantly designed building of mellow sandstone which was erected on the opposite side of the road. Two years later another new branch library of similar construction, although rather larger, was built in Beechwood Road to replace the former library in Moorside School. Gradually, thirteen small service points spread throughout the borough, housed in schools, institutes and Sunday Schools, providing a library service which stretched from Luddenden to Northowram.

Children in the local elementary schools were provided with books from the public libraries until 1906, after which date separate school libraries were established in each school department, and by 1911 about 7,000 specially chosen books were circulating, a figure which had doubled by 1933. It was not until December 1930 that a separate Children's Department was opened at the Central Library with a stock of 5,000 books. In 1908 a popular magazine called *The Satchel* was produced at the Central Library for use in local schools, and carried on until 1947 (Figure 4).

When Edward Green retired on 30 April 1939 after 32 years' fruitful work as Chief Librarian, his place was taken by Frank Haigh,[34] who held the appointment until his death on 7 November 1949. In the same year (1939) Douglas Taylor was appointed as an assistant on 1 July.

The coming of the Second World War inevitably brought many changes; the staff was depleted and those who were not in the armed forces or carrying out war work were faced with the task not only of

Figure 4. Library lesson at Belle Vue Lending Library, 1924. *Calderdale Libraries.*

running the libraries short-handed, but also with the necessity of fire-watching and ARP work.

After Frank Haigh's sudden death, Frank C Pritchard became Chief Librarian on 13 February 1950, continuing in the post until the re-organisation of local government brought into being the new Metropolitan Borough of Calderdale, when he retired and was followed successively by Derek Williamson, Dorothy E Wood and Martin Stone as Chief Librarian of Calderdale. Mr Pritchard was ably assisted by his Deputy, Douglas Taylor, who worked with Halifax Libraries and Calderdale Libraries until his death on 14 November 1978. As a local man Douglas Taylor's knowledge of Halifax history was of great help to many people.

During the 1950s a number of changes were carried out at the Central Library (Figure 5). The former Ladies Reading Room on the first floor was used to accommodate the growing Horsfall Turner Local History Collection, and in the Lending Library the tall

Figure 5. Belle Vue Lending Library, 1960, after partial modernisation.
Calderdale Libraries

Victorian bookcases were reduced in height and modernised, so that the top shelves were brought within easy reach.

A new branch library was opened at King Cross on 3 September 1956 in the former Yorkshire Penny Bank. At first this was on a part-time basis which was soon extended to full-time opening. This was followed on 7 October 1961 by a modern branch library at Mixenden and a similar one at Northowram in June 1966. From about 1956 onwards, various plans for a new Central Library were formulated, and sites considered at the Friendly and Trades Club on St James Road, and on the north side of Broad Street, but these schemes were all rejected.

In 1962 it was decided that as there was insufficient staff to classify the large numbers of new books added to the library, printed catalogue cards should be purchased from the British National Bibliography. One of the later developments in Halifax Libraries was

Figure 6. The Sound and Vision section at Halifax's Central Library today.
John Billingsley

the setting-up of an Archives Department on 20 March 1964[35] with Clifford D Webster, of Leeds, as the first Borough Archivist for Halifax. From a small start this collection has grown to contain millions of documents, some of them hundreds of years old.

In 1974 Halifax County Borough joined with eight other neighbouring authorities to form Calderdale Metropolitan Borough and on 17 January 1983 the new Calderdale Central Library opened on Northgate. The whole system is now on a far greater scale, with a network of district libraries, branch libraries, sub-branches and travelling libraries, covering the whole area from the environs of Todmorden to Brighouse and district, the great tract of territory which once formed the Parish of Halifax.

From the provision of free books and newspapers in 1882, to Calderdale Libraries in 2002 with its once undreamed-of technical resources, its stocks of videos, DVDs and CDs (Figure 6), its computer games and the use of computerised information and printers, photocopiers and fax services, microfilm, fiche and Internet computers (Figure 7), a giant stride forward has taken place. The

Figure 7. Central Reference Library. *John Billingsley*

system continues to grow, to develop, and to move forward using every available new technological device to improve its service to the people of Calderdale, guided by the same spirit which motivated its early planners.

Notes and References

1. T W Hanson, 'Halifax Parish Church Library', *Transactions of the Halifax Antiquarian Society [THAS]*, Halifax, 1951), p 37.
2. W R Barnes and I M Longbotham, *The Story of Halifax Parish Church*, Halifax, n d, p 17.
3. *Halifax Courier*, 14 August 1957.
4. Edward Green, 'Local Libraries: their origin and progress.' *Halifax Guardian Almanack* 1911, p 75.
5. *Ibid.* p 77
6. *Halifax Guardian Almanack,* (1893) p 95.
7. Edward Green, 'Local Libraries: their origin and progress.' *Halifax Guardian Almanack* 1911, p 83.
8. *Ibid.* p 79.
9. *Ibid.*
10. *A Handy Book Descriptive of the Various Institutions in Haley Hill and Copley,* (1865), p 51.
11. *Ibid.* p 97.
12. Edward Green, 'Local Libraries: their origin and progress.' *Halifax Guardian Almanack* 1911, p 83.
13. *Ibid.*

14. *Ibid.* p 87.
15. Letter in Calderdale Central Library. Horsfall Turner Local Studies Collection.
16. *Halifax Courier,* 19 March 1881.
17. Halifax Council Minutes, 6 April 1881.
18. *Ibid.* 15 September 1881.
19. *Ibid.* 6 December 1881.
20. *Ibid.* 14 March 1882.
21. *Ibid.* 10 January 1882.
22. *Ibid.* 29 November 1881.
23. Halifax Public Library. Catalogue and Rules and Regulations. (1882), pp vi-viii.
24. Halifax Council Minutes, 10 October 1882.
25. *Ibid.* 17 December 1883.
26. *Ibid.* 17 January 1882.
27. Halifax Public Libraries. Annual Report, 1886-88, p 3.
28. Halifax Council Minutes, 8 August 1892.
29. Halifax Public Libraries. Annual Report, 1884-85, p 6.
30. *Ibid.* 1885-86, p 5.
31. *Ibid.* 1888-89, p 5.
32. Halifax Council Minutes, 2 November 1894.
33. *Ibid.* 10 September 1906.
34. *Ibid.* 13 March 1939.
35. *Ibid.* 20 March 1964.

11. John Hartley, 'The Yorkshire Burns'

by Aidan Wheelan

THE DIALECT POET, JOHN HARTLEY, was born on 19 October 1839 above a shop on Bedford Street in Halifax. His parents, Rachel and John Hartley, ran a small tea dealership, which was to relocate to Gerrard Street in the late 1840s as they diversified into selling drapery. John's eldest sister, Hannah, seventeen years older than himself, also joined the business as a milliner, though after Rachel's early death Hannah assumed the role of mother to John and his sister Mary.[1]

The youngest of five children, John was a sickly child and before school age had contracted chickenpox, mumps, scarletina and stomach worms. In later life John attributed his survival to the proximity of two druggists, one on either side of his parents' shop. The Hartleys were sufficiently affluent to send the youngster to a 'dame school', the cheapest form of private elementary education, to learn the 3R's.

The awakening of John's egalitarian spirit happened at the early age of seven. His father had taken him to the Halifax Sunday School Jubilee at the Piece Hall, where he lifted the lad on to his shoulders to see the exalted guest, Lord Morpeth, above the crowd. John's first glimpse of aristocracy left him unimpressed. The seeds of 'mi indifference to titled nonentities and mi reverence for labour and genius' were sown.[2]

When old enough, John was dispatched to John Farrar's Classical Academy at 2 Park Place, a middle-class day school. Here John was a lively lad, popular with his peers and excellent at lessons. Yet he was insufficiently deferential towards his Victorian schoolmaster, who beat him frequently. This was, perhaps, the psychological root of his later passionate denunciations of injustice.

Had his family been wealthy John would have sat the Oxbridge entrance examinations. Instead, on leaving school in his teens, John joined James Akroyd and Son at Haley Hill, Halifax,[3] a giant worsted manufactory owned by Edward Akroyd, a noted philanthropist. John began as a junior pattern designer, learning the trade from experienced industrial artists, many of whom were French immigrants. In the evenings John studied design at the new Halifax School of Art.[4] This had been established by Edward Akroyd's initiative in 1859 to improve the standards of indigenous textile design. John probably attended the branch class held at Akroyd's Haley Hill Working Men's College.[5] By his twenty-first birthday John was recognised as a specialist in the design of damasks, in which the pattern is woven, or 'figured', into the fabric and is visible on both sides, not printed on to the material after weaving.

John (Figure 1) married Martha, a Skircoat lass, at Halifax Parish Church on 23 May 1859, and their first child, William, arrived the next year.

In 1856 John had been caught up in the great crowd at the opening of the People's Park near his home. He was struck by a poem circulated at the event in order to eulogise Francis Crossley, the Park's donor. This set John experimenting with 'makkin' verses' for his own amusement.

However, John's real promise shone in the visual arts. In his spare time he painted oils and watercolours, and illuminated manuscripts. Surprisingly for an industrial district, there was at the time much to stimulate artistic

Figure 1. John Hartley, from the frontispiece to *Yorkshire Lyrics*, 1901.

young people around Haley Hill. Opposite John's workplace, between 1856 and 1859, a wealth of creative talent - sculptors, painters, glass designers, metal crafters, woodworkers - had congregated to adorn George Gilbert Scott's masterpiece, All Souls Church. Many of the younger craftsmen joined the School of Art as temporary students. Caught up in the energy of the moment John contributed to the cost of fitting William Wailes' Good Samaritan window into the edifice in honour of Edward Akroyd, his employer.

John's talent for painting pictures with words only came to the fore at what he later described as 'the tragic age of 23', when he read 'Come whoam to thi childer an' me', a poem by the Lancashire dialect poet, Edwin Waugh. Weaned by John Farrar on a diet of Classical and Romantic poetry, Waugh's emotive social realism and melodic use of a northern dialect were a revelation to John Hartley. The language of poetry became immediate and intimate for the first time.

Shortly afterwards John joined the Beacon Club, a young men's social society, wherein each member performed his latest 'party piece' whilst the others downed liquid lubrication. John could neither sing, dance, act, nor play an instrument, but decided he would attempt to translate the spirit of Waugh's popular verses into his own Yorkshire dialect. John's first offering, 'Bite Bigger', the true story of his witnessing two Halifax beggar boys sharing a dirty apple they had found, made a sharp impact on the Beacon Club audience. Despite his manifest hunger, one lad encourages the other to eat more of the apple, with the words 'Nay, tha hasn't taen much, bite again and bite bigger, nah do!'. John Hartley observed that the poor share, they don't compete. He invited his readers to accept this as the same moral challenge he felt it to be at the time. Within weeks a friend had arranged for the piece to be sold in sheet form. Half a century later 'Bite Bigger' was still a favourite recitation at concerts across Yorkshire.

Encouraged, John dashed off more material, much of it set around Halifax and his factory workplace. The prose pieces were witty narratives with West Riding characters, whilst his verses, typically for a young man, were either denunciations of social injustice or accounts of his attraction to young women at the Akroyd's mill - for example, 'Lass O'th Haley Hill'.[6]

Soon John had his first professional engagement, a church 'entertainment' in Shibdendale. John was pre-paid 2s 6d, took the stage after a children's choir, began his reading hesitantly, gained confidence as he went along and only left the platform after giving several encores.

In 1861 John co-founded the Haley Hill Literary and Scientific Society, a high-minded association of educated working men, most attached to Akroyds. He exhibited paintings at the Society's annual soiree, tested out new poems, and explored the history of dialect literature in research papers, for example, on Robert Burns. It was for this Society that John crafted another narrative poem soon to be famous, 'Annie Linn', based on a true story from Heptonstall, his father's birthplace. In 1866 the Society's magazine, *The Circulator*, was the first to publish a series of John Hartley's verses. Other writings went on sale in pamphlet and sheet form, for recitation wherever Yorkshire folk needed a 'party piece'.

Though structurally unoriginal, John's serious poetry did break new ground with its urban and industrial milieu. He consciously rejected the Classical inspiration of most academic poetry:

> *It has not been my lot to pore*
> *O'er the ancient tomes of Classic lore,*
> *Or quaff Castalia's springs;*
> *Yet sometimes the observant eye*
> *May germs of poetry descry,*
> *In plain and common things.*[7]

Instead, poems like 'Lines on Finding A Butterfly in A Weaving Shed' collided the standard Victorian approach to poetry, that is, as observation of Nature, with the 'plain and common things' in the mechanised life of the people of West Yorkshire.[8]

In 'City and Country', John Hartley acknowledged the beauty of Nature but, alluding to All Souls' Church opposite his workplace, he stated his strong preference for synthetic urban culture:

> *I love to see man's power impressed*
> *On the hard rocks that rise,*
> *In tower and spire, hewn, shaped and dressed,*
> *Springing towards the skies.*[9]

The refrain of John's sonnet 'The Short Timer' would have made many middle class readers uncomfortable:

> *Poor lassie wan,*
> *Do th' best tha can,*
> *Although thi fate be hard.*
> *A time ther'll be*
> *When sich as thee*
> *Shall have yor full reward*[10]

John's rejection of Classicism and Romanticism extended to his short stories, His short piece 'True Blue: A Romance of Factory Life' tells of a love rivalry between weavers precipitating a fatal industrial accident.[11]

John's amalgam of witty storytelling, urban realism, and Yorkshire dialect proved astonishingly popular. By the late 1860s his recitations were in demand across the West Riding whilst his writing found new depths of feeling. In 1868 the *Halifax Courier* published 'Shoo's Thi Sister', angrily declaimed after John witnessed a wealthy man push a poor child off a pavement.

> *Gently, gently, shoo's thi sister*
> *Tho' her clooas are nowt but rags.*
> *On her feet ther's monny a blister;*
> *See ha painfully shoo drags*
> *Her tired limbs to some quiet corner.*
> *Shoo's thi sister - dunnot scorn her.*
>
> *Duan her cheeks noa tears are running*
> *Shoo's been shov'd aside befoor*
> *Used to scoffs an' sneers an' shunning*
> *Shoo expects it coss shoo's poor:*
> *Skool'd for years her grief to smother*
> *Still shoo's human, tha'rt her brother.*

Goa thi ways! An if tha bears net
Some regret for what tha's done,
If tha con pass on, an cares net
For that sufferin little one
Then ha'ivver poor shoo be
Yet shoo's rich compared wi thee.[12]

This work demonstrates the compassion and egalitarian protest that was to characterise the best of John's mature work, and make him much more than just a humourist.

1866 proved to be a milestone year for John Hartley on two accounts. That year John and Martha purchased the family's first property, 2 Salisbury Place (Figure 2), one of the first houses in Akroydon Model Village, Edward Akroyd's experiment in low-cost home ownership.[13] The house was a back-to-back terrace on four levels, with an imposing gothic façade. John had saved a £38 deposit on the £338 purchase price, the balance being borrowed from the Halifax Permanent Benefit Building Society.[14] As John was a trusted employee, Edward Akroyd guaranteed the mortgage in order to extend the repayment period from twelve to fifteen years and reduce John's monthly payments. John's new neighbours were mostly fellow members of his Literary and Scientific Society.

A few months later, a young acquaintance, Charles Wilson, jokingly proposed that John write an almanack as a vehicle for his tongue-in-cheek proverbs ('nuggets'),[15] verses, stories and essays ('Ramblin Remarks'), in a similar spirit to modern student magazines. Charles' father, Alfred Wilson, a 'larger-than-life' character weighing twenty-five stones, owned a hat shop at 14 Corn Market, known locally as 'The Clock' after the prominent illuminated timepiece hung over the shop door. The young men, still half in jest, persuaded Alfred to invest the capital for the scheme in

Figure 2. 2 Salisbury Place in 1866, from James Hole, *Homes of the Working Classes*, 1866.

return for publishing rights and control of the title. On 15 October 1866 the first *Illuminated Clock Almanack*, for 1867, went on sale at 2d a copy in Wilson's Hat Shop, Halifax. The initial print-run of 5,000 sold out within a week. The rest, as they say, is history. The youthful joke turned into a publishing legend. John was to write an Almanack every year until his death. Soon average annual sales were around 120,000 and commercial sponsors bought advertising space for such charming period products as 'Williams' Worm Lozenges' and 'Page Woodcock's Wind Pills'.[16]

In the mid-1850s, John's first wife, Martha, died. Within a few years he remarried, this time to Alfred Wilson's daughter, Sophia, thus securing his share in the Almanack's future.

In subsequent years the Almanack (Figure 3) provided both impetus and opportunity for John's literary imagination to flourish. In 1868 the first volume of *Hartley's Yorkshire Ditties*, John's first book, was published and sold well. Then, as now, few authors earned a living wage. John did not give up his 'day job' at Akroyds until late 1871, when he sold 2 Salisbury Place to the Halifax Industrial Society, owner of the 'Co-op' next door. Early in 1872 John invested his savings in a ticket to Quebec by the Allen Line from Liverpool, intending to make his fortune as a performer in the new lands of opportunity.

Whether or not it was naivety that led John, now aged 32, to believe he could earn riches performing Yorkshire dialect pieces on the far side of the Atlantic we can only conjecture. He later admitted to being swept up in a spirit of Bohemianism. Perhaps John was also influenced by his older brother William, who had successfully emigrated from Halifax to South Africa in the early 1850s. Whatever his motivation, after investing most of his savings hiring a hall in Quebec, John gave all 1½ hours of his first performance to a lone paying spectator. He had gambled a good job, a respectable home and a nascent literary reputation, and now was broke.

Undaunted, the Hartleys travelled southwards to Montreal. John never forgave Quebec, later comparing the difference between Montreal and Quebec to that between Saltaire and Salterhebble.[17] Though he found a job as a canvasser for the *Illustrated Canadian News*, it paid the less than princely sum of $5 a week. John and his wife had not

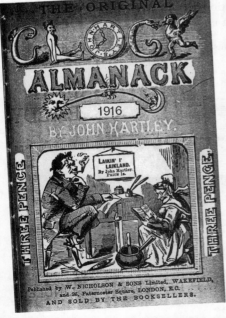

Figure 3. The front cover of the 50th *Anniversary Clock Almanack*.

crossed the Atlantic merely to survive, so they soon moved south into the United States. Drifting through New York, Philadelphia, Buffalo and Washington, John took other menial jobs, gave a few poetry readings, and painted several canvasses, but by 1875 had failed to find any place in the contemporary American literary world.

The *Illuminated Clock Almanack* had survived throughout John's sojourns, his own contributions being fleshed out by other writers, but its popularity was waning without the star author to promote it in person. By the time John returned to live near Chelsea, London, in 1875 Alfred Wilson's widow was only too happy to turn the title over to her son-in-law. Freed from the constraints of commercial sponsorship it was relaunched as simply *The Clock Almanack* by a new publisher, W Nicholson and Sons of Wakefield.

John pursued writing and performing full-time. He entered his most prolific period between 1875 and 1882, creating his literary *alter ego*, Sammywell Grimes, an unsophisticated yet insightful Bradfordian. Sammy and his wife Mally appeared in a series of humorous travelogues, beginning in 1876 with *Seets I' Lundun*. The same year *Yorksher Puddin'*, a collection of short stories, was published. John's American disappointments were recast in comic form in the 1877 volume *Grimes' Trip to America*, ten letters describing the major cities of eastern USA through Yorkshire eyes.

A new departure came early the following year with the publication of *Many A Slip*, a romantic novel, written in standard English, charting the love affairs of three sisters in a weaving mill. Contemporary critics reacted with enthusiasm, praising in particular John's characterisation, but modern readers might find his villain, Grasper, more Dickensian than Dickens, and would wince at the pre-feminist idealised virtue of the delicate, but ever-so-beautiful, heroine, Bella Elmore.

For modern historians the interest of *Many A Slip* lies in the plot's depiction of the benevolent industrialist, the Quaker Mr Thorpe, in counterpoint to the reactionary landowner, Lord Montaine. Against His Lordship's wishes Mr Thorpe constructs a mill in the village, as 'a blessing to the poor round about', ensures the workers are well paid, erects rows of cottages for them, and plants trees to beautify his 'town in miniature'. It is all strongly reminiscent of Akroydon, Copley, and Akroyd's benevolent capitalism. The plot exposes tensions between industry and agriculture, modernity and tradition, technocracy and aristocracy, Dissent and Establishment, the choices behind all nineteenth-century politics. As in his poetry so in his novels, John Hartley votes for change. His preference is underlined

by the novel's dedication to James Stansfeld, the Halifax Radical MP,
a working-class favourite and Unitarian.

The latest Grimes adventures *Seets I' Paris* and *Mally An' Me*,
another romance, *A Rolling Stone* – this time set in Wuthering Heights
territory on the Yorkshire moorlands – a collection of Christmas
Tales, and two volumes of serious pieces, *Pensive Poems and Startling
Stories* and *A Sheaf From The Moorland*, all appeared between 1878
and 1881. Also from about this time, the fifth Grimes adventure,
Seets I' Blackpool, went on sale in 1882.

John returned to Yorkshire in the late 1870s, settling in Brookdale
Terrace, Beeston Hill, Leeds. He now proudly added FSS (Fellow of
the Society of Science, Letters and Arts) and FLS (Fellow of the
Literary Society) to his name. His work sold internationally,
especially to Yorkshire emigrants. The *Wakefield Free Press* described
him as 'The Yorkshire Burns...the man whose literary star is in the
ascendant'. But with celebrity came pressure. John embarked on
seemingly endless and exhausting reading tours around Yorkshire
and further afield. In 1880 he fell seriously ill. When he recovered,
John announced the end of all further public readings.

John's American dream was still unfulfilled. Around 1881 the
Hartleys emigrated from Leeds to Philadelphia, a centre for the
American carpet industry, this time with greater capital and a more
realistic plan. John returned to his Akroyd's training, setting up as a
freelance designer of carpets and upholstery. Soon he found a
business partner, Patrick McCaffery, and was sufficiently successful
to employ his own staff. This freed up time for further writing, but
he had no desire to perform. John continued the Almanack and wrote
more serious poetry, but no further comic or romantic novels were
published while he lived in the USA.

For several years the Hartley family enjoyed an affluent lifestyle
until one week in 1894 John visited his bank to collect the staff wages
only to find its doors bolted. In fact, the whole institution had
collapsed, a less rare occurrence then than now. John lost nearly
everything. Despairing, he managed to sell his business's equipment
in order to fund the fare back to Britain.

The Hartleys returned nearly penniless to Harehills Terrace in
Leeds. They moved to a quieter location, Rose Cottage in Shadwell,
in 1898. The Yorkshire textile industry was in crisis, with both
Akroyds and Salts collapsing. John's only marketable skill was his
writing. Needing popular sales to feed his family, John renewed his
acquaintance with his old friend Sammywell. *Grimes Trip to th' Queen*
came out in 1894. Two years later *Seets I' Yorkshire and Lancashire*,

Sammy's description of the Leeds to Liverpool Canal, was published, and in 1899 John edited a retrospective of his dialect poetry, issued in 1901 as *Yorkshire Lyrics*. Emotionally John took solace in his relationship with his young daughter Annie, whom he adored.

Against his better judgement John returned to reading tours. Though the public welcomed back their old favourite Grimes and crowded back into John's performances, he was to pass the rest of his life in comparative poverty and increasing ill health. On 13 January 1902, now aged 62, John collapsed seriously ill during a reading at the Holborn Restaurant, London. He did not reappear in public for over seven years. Other than the Almanack, John completed little written work in this period. His public missed him. In 1910 his publishers were forced to issue denials of John Hartley's death to counter persistent rumours.

In his 1905 poem 'The Fall of The Curtain' we find John contemplating his disappointments and his mortality:

> *I mourn as the increasing years compel*
> *Retirement from the rush of worldly strife,*
> *I grieve to find weakness and pains foretell*
> *The closing scene of erstwhile busy life.*
>
> *Unsatisfied ambitions mock my rest*
> *Filling my heart with sad and vain regret,*
> *I plead, 'I humbly tried my best'.*
> *Time and strength failed me - soon the sun will set.*[18]

In April 1907 John briefly returned to Akroydon for the funeral of his former Akroyd's colleague, and fellow freemason, Edward Halliday.[19] The next month John was elected Honorary Life Fellow of the Yorkshire Literary Society. In 1909 John and his second wife moved to Liscard on the Wirral for the sea air. Here they could stroll down to New Brighton Promenade to watch the Atlantic liners setting sail to their former North American home. For financial reasons alone John recommenced a limited number of public readings.

This creatively dry period ended in 1911 with a fresh comic adventure, *Grimes and Mally Laikin I' Lakeland*. The third volume of his *Yorkshire Tales* was released in 1913. A revised edition of *Yorkshire Lyrics* was published, this time with the endorsement of both the King and Queen. Royal approval focused educated attention on to the ageing author. His friend of many years, Charles Forshaw of Bradford,[20] wrote an appreciation of John's work, and, to mark John's seventieth birthday in 1909, convened an 'honorary dinner' at the

Great Northern Hotel, Bradford, at which John was presented with a portrait of himself. Three years later a similar event was held in his hometown on his birthday. On this occasion John received an illuminated address and a purse of gold. He was frail and prone to depression, but still able to recite 'Bite Bigger' with all its original pathos. In 1913 the Society of Yorkshiremen in London, following the earlier examples, hosted a banquet in John's honour.

Concern was raised about John's health and material circumstances. Neuritis had inflamed his limbs, leaving him lame and, more crucially for a professional writer, unable to hold a pen. A body of prominent men, barristers, politicians, authors, academics and magistrates, petitioned the Treasury to grant John Hartley a Civil List pension. But even if this had been successful John was obstinately independent, a common Yorkshire trait. He refused all offers of help until his final year when he accepted a five-shilling a week annuity from a group of friends.

John's second wife died in January 1914. Their marriage had lasted over forty years. Within a few months John had proposed marriage by letter to an old Hebden Bridge friend, Annie Spencer, also a dialect poet, who was teaching in Vancouver. When in September that year Annie returned to England, the couple were married at the Birkenhead registry office (Figure 4). In 1914 John had, against to his own expectations, completed the 50th Anniversary (1916) edition of his *Almanack*. Early in 1915 John and Annie set about writing the 1917 *Almanack* together. It was to be the last work of John's literary career.

On 18 December 1915, two months after the 50th *Clock Almanack* went on sale, John Hartley died of heart failure following pneumonia at his home at 11 Sea View Avenue, Liscard. He left four sons, a daughter, and over 400 published works. He was widely mourned, and amongst reports of the slaughter of the Great War most newspapers found space for an obituary.[21]

In his poem 'When The End Comes', John Hartley had requested:

> *Lay me not down with a sculptured stone*
> *To press heavily on my breast:*
> *Let my coverlet be the yielding loam*
> *In nature's green mantle drest.*

> *Lay me not down where the willow's tears*
> *Shall gloomily fall on my bed;*
> *But put me to sleep where the wild flowers creep,*
> *Making bright the dark home of the dead.*[22]

In the event, John was buried at Wallasey Cemetery. His funeral was a quiet affair, with only his daughter, Annie Moore, her husband, their son and John's close friend Charles Forshaw present.

The *Clock Almanack* did not die with John Hartley, but was taken up by other dialect enthusiasts, in particular Walter Hampson, and survived until the Second World War.

Our nearest contemporary parallel to John Hartley is, perhaps, Roger McGough, a writer in many media and moods, a distinctive northern voice and a popular performer, with a flair for comedy perversely rewarded by academic neglect of his more emotive and perceptive work. Had John Hartley not written in dialect, had he moderated his social commentary, and had he not penned the Grimes series, then perhaps the literary establishment would have showered more honours on him.

Figure 4. A late photograph of John Hartley. *Calderdale Libraries*

What is less understandable is that John's home townsfolk seem to have forgotten his existence. Though his books are available at the Halifax library, there is no plaque, no road or building named after him, and no mention in the town's history books. Even the bust presented to Belle Vue Library by admirers after his death has been lost. John himself would have been phlegmatic about this. Around 1904 he had revisited his birthplace in Bedford Street. He wrote:

> *This is the street, here stands the cot,*
> *The cot where I was born,*
> *Its inmates stare - they know me not,*
> *Its aspect is forlorn.*
> *It looks so small, so dull, so old,*
> *So changed - yet still the same,*
> *I feel my heart's blood running cold*
> *I turn away in sharne.*
>
> *Yet this had been my happy home,*
> *Where childhood's days were passed.*
> *And I have traveled far to come*
> *And find it thus at last.*
> *Imagination pictured it*
> *So cosy, bright and clean,*
> *But what my fancy painted it*
> *It never could have been.*[23]

Notes and References

1. Two other siblings, William and Anne, had left home by the 1851 Census.
2. *The Clock Almanack* 1891, p 34.
3. Now the site of Avena Carpets.
4. Now incorporated into Calderdale College as the School of Integrated Arts.
5. Situated on the north side of the junction of Range Lane and Haley Hill.
6. *Yorkshire Lyrics*, Nicholson, London, 1901, p 214.
7. *Yorkshire Lyrics*, Nicholson, London, 1901, frontispiece.
8. *Yorkshire Lyrics*, Nicholson, London, 1901, p 131.
9. *The Clock Almanack* 1880.
10. *Yorkshire Lyrics*, Nicholson, London, 1901, p 43.
11. *Yorkshire Tales, Third Series*, Nicholson, London, 1913.
12. *Halifax Weekly Courier*, 1868.
13. Edward Akroyd and his brother Henry had already built Copley Model Village between 1847 and 1851.
14. Now 'The Halifax plc'.
15. For example, 'A fair face an' a faal heart is like a clean dicky an' a mucky shirt.' Or 'Temperance is a gooid principle to stick to, even in teetotalism.'
16. The cartoon covers of the *Clock Almanack*, along with those of the Grimes series, are believed to be the only remaining examples of John Hartley's artwork. The *Almanack* cover shows an old couple from the days of domestic spinning in their cottage with their spindle cast aside whilst they read and write. Above the sun and the moon are pulling tongues at each other.
17. Salterhebble is the site of the Halifax Sewage Works.
18. *The Clock Almanack 1907*.
19. John Hartley dedicated the second edition of Yorkshire Ditties to Halliday's brother-in-law, Richard Cherry, another old friend from Salisbury Place in Akroydon.
20. Charles Forshaw, also a Yorkshire poet, edited the magazine *Yorkshire Notes and Queries* and introduced John Hartley to Freemasonry.
21. *Halifax Evening Courier*, 18 December 1915, and *Halifax Guardian*, 24 December 1915.
22. Charles Forshaw, *Yorkshire Poets Volume 1*, Bradford, 1888.
23. *The Clock Almanack 1905*.

12. 'Archaeology of The Mouth': Ted Hughes and His Birth-Place

by John Billingsley

THERE ARE FEW WRITERS whose work is so closely tied in with Calderdale's landscape as Ted Hughes, the late Poet Laureate. In Hughes' verse we are led to an engagement with the experience of place that seems to have owed much in inspiration to his early childhood in the upper valley. From his poems, particularly in *Remains of Elmet*, but also scattered throughout his other collections, we can pick up threads that will lead us in this article through the recreation of a formative map.

The end-terrace house in which Ted Hughes was born would not seem to have been the perfect setting for any poet, let alone one who would become for many essentially a poet of the wild places, both in nature and personality. At his end of the terrace, the houses were not back-to-back, but 1 Aspinall Street (Figure 1) in Mytholmroyd's Banksfield neighbourhood exits on to a narrow alley, the back door confronted by another just ten feet away. The front windows looked

Figure 1. Ted Hughes' birthplace. 1 Aspinall Street, Mytholmroyd; his bedroom window was the upper one in the gable end. *John Billingsley*

Figure 2. Ted's parents, Billy and Edith (née Farrer). *Lloyd Greenwood*

out on to a square of rough land, known then as Plot Ground, as it was on this patch of land that the neighbourhood's November bonfire would be lit. Around it, rows of terraced houses formed a kind of box; Jubilee Street (misspelt Jubillee Street on the official sign) to the right and Banksfield Street to the left. Above these, capping the box, was the low roof of Helliwell's Mill at the top of the slope.

There was no view from the left of the house, joined as it is to the Aspinall Street row, where other relatives, on his mother's side, lived in a local concentration of family members (Figures 2, 3 & 4) far more common then than now. Ted's aunt, Hilda Farrar, lived at No. 13 and his uncle Albert at No. 19. To the right, though, dominating the view from young Edward's bedroom, was the Mount Zion chapel.

Figure 3. A very young Ted with his father, Billy Hughes. *Lloyd Greenwood*

Figure 4. Ted (right) with brother Gerald and sister Olwyn. *Lloyd Greenwood*

This is the only outlook from that house which has significantly changed from that day, 17 August 1930, when Edward James Hughes was born, as Keith Sagar put it, 'deep in a sodden valley of the Yorkshire Pennines'.[1] Today, the chapel has been replaced with a small block of flats whose stone is somewhat brighter than the walls of the chapel. Some local historians now recall it as a handsome building, as indeed it appears in old photographs (Figure 5); but for Hughes, born and first raised literally in its shadow, as it lay between

Figure 5. Mount Zion chapel before demolition. The Hughes house can be seen immediately to its left in the picture. The old Midgley Road bridge in the foreground was known as Navvy Bridge. *Donald Crossley Collection*

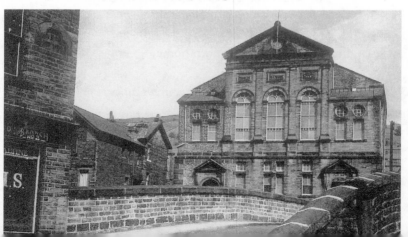

him and the morning light, it held less fond memories.

> *Blackness was a building blocking the moon ...*
> *that uplifted mass*
> *Was a deadfall*
> *He would be taken there on Sundays,*
> *gripped by elders*
> *Like a jibbing calf* [2]

and his poem reads like early confirmation that neither religion nor his spirit could be confined by walls and 'Moses mouthings'.

If the chapel was like a prison, lifting his eyes beyond it only revealed another wall - the great cliff scar of Hathershelf Scout Rock, which, though attractive on a sunny summer day, looms dark and morose against the winter sun or in dank misty weather. All around, the walls of Mytholmroyd are stained black with the sooty legacy of its industrial history, stippled and striped by

> *acid rain fall-out*
> *From Manchester's rotten lung.* [3]

However, Ted could escape from that wall by going in the opposite direction, along to the far end of Aspinall Street, past Mrs Wellock's corner shop at the foot of Albert Street, down towards the canal and past the dyehouse (now the *Redacre Mill Hotel*) to the woods and the tangle of tree and scrub that fronted the worked-out quarry behind Redacre Farm. This area could also be accessed from where the post-war prefabs now stand, on what was known as the Co-op Fields, home to chicken pens and allotments. At the foot of these fields, still visible today, a stone-paved track led 'down t'slope'. This area offered the sense of the wild to Ted and his playmates - Derek Robertshaw, Donald Crossley and Brian Seymour were the usual gang - and indeed it still does to local children. Back 'on t'top' in the fields, Ted and his Uncle Albert played traditional northern sports:

> *He and I*
> *Lammed our holly billets across Banksfields -*
> *A five-inch propeller climbing the skylines*
> *For two, three seconds - to the drop*

At least until Albert died in his own home,

> *When he tripped*
> *The chair from beneath him, in his attic*

Ted's sometimes acute sensitivity apparently ran in the family, for as

her brother hanged himself,

> *his sister, forty miles off*
> *Cried out at the hammer blow on her nape*[4]

Another way out of the box of houses was to duck beneath the 'wall' of chapel and Scout Rock, figuratively at least, and run 'down t'clough' to the towpath of the Rochdale Canal. A flight of steps led to it from beside the old Co-op on Midgley Road; they still do, although the 'navvy bridge' was totally rebuilt when Midgley Road was doubled in width. One attraction would be a visit to another uncle, Walter Farrar, who lived on the edge of the village at Southfield, easily and safely accessible by the towpath; Hughes got on well with Walt, and regularly returned to stay with him in later years.

Another canal attraction was the contrast it offered to the view from Hughes' window; a world view so dominated by stone would meet there a world of water, an altogether more playful element - whereas the land he could see changed its mood slowly through weather and light, and people moved in perpetual mourning, and crows flapped slowly over the stone, here in the water fish darted and jumped, and the reflected landscape broke and rippled in response. Later in life, Hughes was as lyrical about fish as he was about land, and it is tempting to see the roots of his love of fishing in this contrasting world of the canal depths.

Of course, the canal was no game-fishing venue - but it was perfect for a boy and a net made out of kitchen curtaining, dangled close to the stone banks, enticing the 'torpid, ginger-bearded, secretive' loach, with their 'little cupid mouths', to bolt from their stone hideyholes into the net and thence to a large jam-jar on a windowsill.

But the jam-jar on the windowsill was not their element, and the canal soon received their stiff corpses. From a poem in Remains of Elmet, one can picture the young boy standing on the roadside below his home, high over the canal,

> *Mount Zion's*
> *Cowled, Satanic Majesty*
> *behind me,*[3]

'lobbing' the dead fish back into the dark water, *'their Paradise and mine'* (Figure 6).

Figure 6. The bank from which Ted lobbed his unfortunate catch back into the canal. *John Billingsley*

Figure 7. The 'Long Tunnel Ceiling', under the A646. *John Billingsley*

Indeed, dead fish were not the only objects tossed from that high bank - an old playmate, Donald Crossley, has recalled how, on their way to their Burnley Road school, they would bombard the roof of the Empress Foundry, across the canal, with stones. The long single-storey mill was derelict at that time, with rosebay willow-herb and even trees growing inside, nurtured by the 'huge light' falling though its impressive array of large skyward windows; these panes, passively sunbathing on the roof, were just too much temptation.

The dark water and the blackened bridges of the canal were a conduit out of the mundane into another world of experience. A hundred yards east of the Midgley Road 'Navvy Bridge', where Hughes most quickly accessed the towpath, was another bridge, longer, almost a tunnel; he and his friends called it 'the long tunnel' - here 'was the place for dark loach' (Figure 7).[5] Hughes was not the only intruder - there was a day when 'a trout nearly as long as my arm' jumped within this dark echoey space, astounding the boy:

> *a brick*
> *Rose through its eruption - hung massive*
> *Then slammed back with a shock and a shattering*

This grand fish was clearly a cut above the loach, it was a dismissive 'free lord' in its new world, and it excited in Hughes a train of thought that envisioned it brought down from the hills in thunderous rain that burst the streams. It was more than a lord - it was

> *a seed*
> *Of the wild god now flowering for me*[5]

that called to the boy from somewhere far removed from his semi-urban home; and perhaps years later in a remote pool in the Highlands he met the wild god again, this time a salmon -

> *the pool lifted a travelling bulge*
> *And grabbed the tip of my heart-nerve, and crashed.*[6]

Such a similar experience, separated by decades and the transcendence of the dark memories of childhood.

So the canal and the road hinted at a way out of what Hughes called the 'shadow trap' of the valley - laden lorries rumbled busily east and west to Halifax and Lancashire, albeit the latter not without its 'grisly false start at Todmorden',[7] but that farther-distant world was to come later in life for Ted. For the young boy, escape still had to be found within the small world of his immediate community, and a route of escape was suggested by his reflection on the trout's progress.

When you're down, the only way out is up, and two directions were open to him. Hughes recalls the landscape of his birth, and his emergence from it, most forcefully in an essay called 'The Rock', which prefigures the close identification with the local landscape that can be seen, years later, in Remains of Elmet and in between in poems in other collections. One way up and out was across the river and up the side of Hathershelf Scout, outflanking rather than confronting the forbidding cliff that he felt to be a 'memento mundi over my birth; my spiritual midwife at the time and my godfather ever since'.[7]

Scout Rock is the scar left by an ancient landslip, its near-vertical face softened in summer by clumps of trees and bushes, its foot littered with chunks of fallen rock (and now, as a legacy of a council tip, asbestos waste). Among those rocks was found in 1951 a Roman coin hoard - probably hidden there by some thieving Briton who hoped that the rock's forbidding aspect would be proof against its discovery. He was right, and it was only through a dog on a rabbiting expedition that the hoard was found, nearly 2,000 years later.[8]

The Rock, thought Hughes, cast its own personality on to local society:

> *that cliff was both the curtain and back-drop to existence. All that happened, happened against it or under its supervision.... It was a darkening presence, like an over-evident cemetery. Living beneath it was like living in a house haunted by a disaster that nobody can quite believe ever happened, though it regularly upsets sleep'.*[7]

He felt himself hemmed in by it - more than that, its presence somehow sealed the local community in its sense of dissatisfaction and a melancholy for the Great War, to which local men had gone in the command of the Lancashire Fusiliers, and only a handful had returned. One of that handful was Hughes' father, reputedly saved only by the passbook in his pocket, but silent on his wartime experiences.[9] More communicative was his Uncle Walt, who recalled how, wounded and trapped in a French shell-hole by a sniper, he visualised his home and

> *went walks,*
> *Along the Heights Road, from Peckett to Midgley,*
> *Down to Mytholmroyd (past Ewood*
> *Of his ancestors, past the high-perched factory*
> *Of his future life) Up the canal bank,*
> *Up Redacre, along and down into Hebden ...*
> *... - all day*
> *He walked about the valley, as he lay*
> *Under High Wood in the shell-hole.*[10]

Around the child in the 1930s, the valley mourned its losses, and survivors remembered; like his father, who would never talk about the war, but at night, dreamed:

> *The whole hopelessness still going on,*
> *No man's land still crying and burning*
> *inside our house...*[11]

Economic privation and melancholy were doubtless at that time a potent influence on valley life, and they were not helped in Mytholmroyd by Scout Rock, which soured Hughes to valleys:

> *It should have inured me to living in valleys, or gulleys, or under walls,*

but all it did was cause me to hate them. The slightest declivity now makes me uneasy and restless, and I slip into the shadow of the mood of that alley - a foreboding heaviness, such as precedes downpour thunderstorms on Sunday afternoons.[7]

So it certainly wasn't up that hill that Hughes climbed to be free of the sense of oppression that came and went in the valley, but it was the strip of green above Helliwell's Mill that beckoned to him and his playmates.

Escape from the shadow trap was ...north and upwards, up the north slope to the moors ... I must have been quite young, three or four, when I started my walks to the moors.[7]

Over-protective parents today would surely and sadly not allow three-year-olds the kind of freedom that doubtless fired Hughes' later creativity.

Before Banksfield Estate was built, the field-path began just above the mill, at the Co-op Fields. One can still follow the line of that path, preserved as walkways between the houses, leading to a stile and then into the higher fields, and the atmosphere of the climb, once among the fields, is not so different from Hughes' day (Figure 8). It is a toiling climb straight up to the magnificent, but now lamentably neglected, Birchen Lee Carr. However, as each field-wall, or its remains, are reached, there is a clear sense of another step being taken out of the valley; for me this sensation is unequalled anywhere else in upper Calderdale, perhaps because the fields are a regular size, and as one naturally pauses to look back the way one has come, the gradation of the ascent is clearly recognised. Looking out

Figure 8. This photograph, taken before Helliwell's Mill was built, clearly shows how the footpath led straight uphill, drawing Hughes' imagination with it up towards the moors. *Calderdale Libraries*

over the rooftops of Mytholmroyd at the hills across the valley, there is a paradox - although the hills one sees are physically further away, they seem closer, and steadily closer as we climb and look back; and find a new incentive to resume the steep pull uphill, towards the moor. The effect on the mind is like peeling off layers of an onion - the closer you get to the heart, the more it gets to you.

I met this sensation when I moved to Mytholmroyd in 1975, and a few years later, when a friend introduced me to 'The Rock', I realised that Hughes seemingly had a much similar feeling about this hillside. The experience and perception is not unique, but a characteristic of the place itself. Just as Scout Rock pinned the valley down, made it aware of its fixity, this path opens one to the totally different atmosphere of the moors.

> *From the very start, the moors were the exciting destination... a thousand distractions tended to draw me off along the slope, among the woods and lanes and farms,*

but it isn't far up the hill before, looking back,

> *you saw that the ridge of Scout Rock was a ridge below the further ridge of moor, and moor was friendly.*[7]

The path emerges on to the Birchen Lee Carr driveway, lined by tall sycamores (Figure 9), and it seems an avenue to another, older

Figure 9. The Birchen Lee Carr driveway continued Hughes' upward ascent. *John Billingsley*

world; on this shelf of land lies a hamlet of old farms and it is this shelf of land where Mytholmroyd finally dips below the line of sight. The moors are suddenly closer -

> *Landscapes gliding blue as water*
> *Those barrellings of strength are heaving slowly and heave*
> *To your feet and surf upwards*
> *In a still, fiery air, hauling the imagination.*[12]

Steadily toiling upward, one gets to another place of Hughes' memory -

> *The Heights Road, my brother launching a glider,*
> *Just below where an airplane crashed by the golf-links ...*
> *And the first hawk I ever saw and knew*
> *Flew past with a small bird in its claw.*[13]

and still the young boy's climb proceeds, on to Midgley Moor. It takes him to the standing stone, no prehistoric menhir, but a tall boundary stone known mysteriously as Churn Milk Joan (Figure 10), and the subject of another poem in *Remains of Elmet*.[14] Folklore draws to this stone like moths -

> *A lonely stone*
> *Afloat in the stone heavings of emptiness*
> *Keeps telling her tale.*

Joan, so the story goes, was a milkmaid from Mount Skip who died at the spot in inclement weather - but how? The version I heard was that she dropped dead in the snow; but Hughes heard that 'Foxes killed her'. Hughes knew too of the plague stone tradition now associated with Churn Milk Joan, by which

> *You take the coins out of the hollow in the top of it.*
> *Leave your own in*

to ensure good fortune in the coming year. Did he, like other Mytholmroyd children of his generation, join hands with his companions and circle the stone, making a wish?[15] And had he heard that the stone turns thrice at midnight at New Year, when it hears St Michael's bells ring in Mytholmroyd?

Near Churn Milk Joan is a line of what look like ruined huts, but these are grouse-butts,

> *the front-line emplacements of a war nearly religious...*
> *A religion too arcane*
> *For the grouse*[16]

Figure 10. 'A lonely stone...'. Churn Milk Joan, with Crow Hill behind. *John Billingsley*

Once again we feel we are in a landscape where the divine is ever-potential - even 'the sluttiest sheep in England' are 'angels ...in the likeness of beggars',[17] aptly enough where

> *Moors*
> *Are a stage for the performance of heaven.*[18]

Looking down on the stone and butts is Crow Hill (Figure 10), also featured in Hughes' work[19] and one wonders if the crows of the valley, ubiquitous in nature and place-name, inspired his quasi-shamanic poem cycle, *Crow*. Walking on Midgley and Wadsworth Moors, one is never far away from the perceptions that fed into the Elmet collection, nor from the influences that fed Hughes' interest in shamanism and myth.

The moors exerted a powerful influence on Hughes - 'after each visit I must have returned less and less of myself to the valley',[7] until

Figure 11. The commemorative plaque affixed to Hughes' birthplace. Part of Scout Rock can be seen in the background. *John Billingsley*

when he was eight his family moved to Mexborough in South Yorkshire, ending a crucial formative phase for the young Edward Hughes. The social world he grew up in is barely recognisable today, though it can be visualised in his equally rich poetry about his family and other characters of the valley. Physically, though, Hughes' childhood world is still very much with us, and through poetry and the power of place it can come alive if one walks through the Banksfield neighbourhood and up to the moors.

Maps have no beginnings, but paths do, and in this word-map of the Mytholmroyd vicinity we can follow Hughes on a path of play, by the canal at the foot of the valley, through aspiration climbing up the slopes of Banksfield, to release on the moors, and it is no surprise that it was in such terrain - albeit Dartmoor, nearer his final home than Midgley Moor - that Hughes willed his ashes to be scattered. If moors are really a stage for the performance of heaven, then one can imagine him there now, giving the performance of his life.

> *From now on the land*
> *Will have to manage without him.*[20]

Notes and References

The title of this article comes from the introductory poem to *Remains of Elmet*.

1. Sagar, Keith. *The Art of Ted Hughes*, Cambridge University Press, 1978, p 6.
2. 'Mount Zion', *Remains of Elmet (RE)* (1979).
3. 'The Canal's Drowning Black', *RE*.
4. 'Sacrifice', *Wolfwatching* (1989).
5. 'The Long Tunnel Ceiling', *RE*.
6. 'Milesian Encounter on the Sligachan', *River* (1983).
7. 'The Rock', *Worlds*. Penguin, 1974.
8. 'Hoard of Roman Coins Found at Mytholmroyd', *The Elphin* No 1, 1991 (Mytholmroyd Historical Society)
9. See 'For the Duration' and 'Dust As We Are', *Wolfwatching*.
10. Sagar, Keith (ed.). *The Achievement of Ted Hughes*. Manchester University Press, 1983, p 9; 'Walt', *Wolfwatching*.
11. 'For the Duration', *Wolfwatching*.
12. 'Pennines in April', *Lupercal* (1960).
13. 'What's the First Thing You Think of?', *Elmet* (1994).
14. 'Churn Milk Joan', *RE*.
15. Pers. comm., members of the Mytholmroyd Historical Society, 1995.
16. 'Grouse-Butts', *RE*.
17. 'The Sluttiest Sheep in England', *RE*.
18. 'Moors', *RE*.
19. 'Crow Hill', *Lupercal*.
20. 'The Day He Died', *Moortown Diary* (1989).

Acknowledgments

My sincere thanks are due to Donald Crossley for sharing his memories of his Banksfield childhood with me, and Frank Woolrych and Lloyd Greenwood for the Hughes family photos.

Postscript

Hughes held his memories of Banksfield longer than Banksfield held his. I moved into Jubilee Street in 1975, while Hughes was compiling *Remains of Elmet*, and soon learned that he had been born in the neighbourhood. I asked my ageing neighbours where, but I obviously wasn't asking the right people - the reliability of the answers can be gauged by the fact that it wasn't until the publication of the book in 1979 that I was finally able, through following the clear clues contained in the poems, to identify Hughes' birthplace as No.1.

Now the breach in communal memory has been plugged by a small black plaque affixed to the corner of the house on 6 February 1993 (Figure 11). Aptly, it faces uphill, towards the moor-bound footpath.

CONTRIBUTORS

12. ARCHAEOLOGY OF THE MOUTH: TED HUGHES AND HIS BIRTHPLACE

John Billingsley has lived in the upper Calder valley since 1975, and has developed a keen interest in its landscape and lore. He has worked for Calderdale Libraries since 1990, and has edited the neo-antiquarian magazine, *Northern Earth*, since 1992. He lectures part-time in Pennine folklore and cultural tradition at Bradford University, and is also a freelance speaker and writer. He has published *A Stony Gaze* (Capall Bann, 1998), a book deriving from his Sheffield University MA thesis on West Yorkshire's carved stone heads, and *The Day the Sun Went Out* (Northern Earth, 1999), about the 1927 solar eclipse in Yorkshire.

10. FROM QUILL TO COMPUTER

Derek Bridge was born in Halifax and educated at Heath Grammar School, after which his interest in literature prompted him to join the staff of Halifax Public Library and study for qualification as a chartered librarian. For 37 years he was Reference Librarian with Halifax, and later Calderdale, Public Libraries, during which time his work in the field of local history led him to the Halifax Antiquarian Society, to which he has contributed articles, and in which he is now Publications Officer. In 1988 he collaborated with Dr Alan Betteridge and Peter Thornborrow to publish *Calderdale Architecture and History,* and in 1991 he and Dr Betteridge published *Maps and*

Views of Old Halifax. He has written an article on Edwards of Halifax, for the *New Dictionary of National Biography.* He is married and has a son and a daughter, both married.

4. HEARTS, CIRCLES, DIAMONDS AND SCROLLS

David Cant was born and brought up in Eastbourne, East Sussex. His interest in local history was aroused while living in Norfolk, and when he moved to Yorkshire in 1986 he became particularly interested in buildings and architecture. He was chair of the Yorkshire Vernacular Buildings Study Group for five years and is actively involved in the Vernacular Architecture Group of the Halifax Antiquarian Society. His interest in the decoration of seventeenth century houses is part of a continuing study of local buildings. Publications include articles on the Jackson family, woodcarvers, of Coley; contributions to *Yorkshire Buildings,* the *Journal of the Yorkshire Vernacular Buildings Study Group*; and the *Guide to the Industrial Heritage of West Yorkshire.*

1. THE EARLY PREHISTORY OF CALDERDALE

Michael Robert Haigh was born in Halifax in 1955, and his early years were rather nomadic before he settled down in Mytholmroyd in the early 1970s. An early interest in science led him to pursue a career in chemistry at a time when most industries that require chemists were going into decline. A suitable degree was obtained from Queen Mary College, London, where he also picked up an interest in archaeology. Back in Calderdale, he was employed by Samuel Webster's Brewery and joined the Yorkshire Archaeological Society, and he has been looking back ever since. He writes a regular archaeology column for *Northern Earth* magazine.

7. GUNS AND ROSES: BENJAMIN WILSON OF SALTERHEBBLE

John A Hargreaves, born in Burnley, has lived in Calderdale since 1972. He was educated at Burnley Grammar School and Southampton University, where he wrote a dissertation on Chartism for his BA Honours degree and also completed a postgraduate Certificate of Education. He subsequently obtained an MA with distinction and PhD at Huddersfield University for a thesis exploring the relationship between religion and society in the parish of Halifax from the eighteenth century to the twentieth century. He has taught history for over thirty years and is currently Head of Humanities at a comprehensive school in Batley. He served as secretary of the Halifax Antiquarian Society for fifteen years and is currently President of the society and Editor of its Transactions. He has lectured extensively on local history and contributed to radio and television documentaries. His numerous publications include *Halifax*, a full-length history of the town published by Edinburgh University Press/Carnegie Publishing in 1999 and pictorial histories of Halifax and Sowerby Bridge, published by Smith Settle. He is a Fellow of the Royal Historical Society.

3. A QUESTION OF ATTRIBUTION: NATHAN FIELDING AND HIS VIEWS OF HALIFAX FROM HALEY HILL

Nigel Herring has worked with Calderdale Museums as Curator of the art collections since local government reorganisation in 1974. His background is in architecture and art history, with a B Arch and M A respectively from Edinburgh. He is passionate about art and design of the twentieth century and aspects of local history. His alter ego is Henry Cockerlin, butler to Edward Ackroyd at Bankfield.

2. THE DEVELOPMENT OF NORTH BRIGHOUSE 1790-1910

David Nortcliffe has lived in the Brighouse area all his life. His particular interest is the story of the town and village development over the past four centuries. In his 'spare' time he is studying for a degree in the History of Science & Technology. For many years he worked in the Countryside Services of West Yorkshire CC and Calderdale MBC, which enabled him to gather additional material regarding our rural heritage. He is a member of Halifax Antiquarian Society of almost thirty years' standing, having been on its committee for several years, and a member of the Yorkshire Archaeological Society, where he was Chairman of its Industrial Section for a time. He is also a Tourist Guide for Calderdale. His main published works have been in relation to Kirklees Hall where he proved the John Carr involvement with the important flying staircase, and showed that the estate had an Iron Bridge a decade before the one at Coalbrookdale.

6. WHEN THE CHIEFS CAME TO TOWN

Jill Robinson lives in Luddenden Foot with her teenage son, Alex. She has worked as a researcher at several universities, and also for a number of voluntary sector organisations in West Yorkshire. Jill spent some time in the Southern African state of Botswana, formerly known as Bechuanaland, where she became interested in the country's history and literature. She has contributed articles and chapters to a variety of publications, and her first novel, *Berringden* Brow was published in 2001.

5. JAMES ALDERSON, BREWERY PROPRIETOR

Peter W Robinson was born in Huddersfield, but has always resided in Halifax where he received his education, first at Warley Road School and then at Heath Grammar School. He was articled at Messrs Bousfield Waite & Co, chartered accountants, worked briefly at Allied Mills in Brighouse, then took up his present employment in the Finance Department of the Nestlé Rowntree Division of Nestlé UK Ltd, Halifax. He has been the Treasurer of the Halifax Antiquarian Society since 1989. With a long-tanding interest in the local brewing industry, he has edited two CAMRA local beer guides and written several articles on local breweries, including a specially commissioned history of the Fountain Head Brewery. Other published work includes a three-part study of public baths and bathing in Calderdale, the Yorkshire stone square system of fermentation, and the career of local architect Joseph F Walsh.

8. LADY BEHIND THE LENS

Issy Shannon. Following a career in journalism spanning over forty years, on newspapers ranging from the *Manchester Evening News* and *Gloucester Citizen* to the *Rochdale Observer* and *Ross-on-Wye Gazette,* Issy Shannon is now enjoying a retirement free from the demands of 'new technology'. Her last post was on the *Hebden Bridge Times,* where for five years she wrote a weekly feature entitled 'The Longstaff Collection'. It is her ambition to continue writing on the life of Hebden Bridge photographer Alice Longstaff - and avoid becoming a 'silver surfer' at all costs!

9. THE WARLEY MAYPOLE

Garry Stringfellow was born in Halifax in 1947 and currently lives in Sowerby Bridge. Now a retired teacher, he has had a variety of occupations but he has always lived and worked in Calderdale. For almost forty years he has had more than a passive interest in folk traditions and local history. Through this and his interest and involvement in traditional dance, he was in 1977 instrumental in the revival of the rushbearing festival in Sowerby Bridge. He continues to dance with groups in Yorkshire and Lancashire, and he is still involved in the doings of Sowerby Bridge through his involvement with different community groups.

11. JOHN HARTLEY, 'THE YORKSHIRE BURNS'

Aidan Whelan. Born in Northern England, Aidan Whelan took his degree at Durham University. After working in London housing estates in the late 1980s, he settled in Halifax in 1991. Since then he has worked on social housing projects in Bradford, Sheffield, Hull, Elland, Dewsbury and Huddersfield. He is a Practitioner of the Chartered Institute of Housing and an Associate of the Chartered Institute of Personnel and Development. His interest in housing history led him to write the historical texts for the 'Home From The Mill' exhibition, a celebration of Akroydon Model Village, in 1995, still on display in Bankfield Museum, Halifax. Aidan, a Quaker, lives quietly with his wife in Akroydon. His free time is devoted to preparing a biography of Edward Akroyd.

INDEX